P9-CQQ-307

MANHATTAN PREP

Algebra

GMAT Strategy Guide

This essential guide covers algebra in all its various forms (and disguises)
on the GMAT. Master fundamental techniques and nuanced strategies to
help you solve for unknown variables of every type.

guide **2**

Algebra GMAT Strategy Guide, Sixth Edition

10-digit International Standard Book Number: 1-941234-00-3
13-digit International Standard Book Number: 978-1-941234-00-6
eISBN: 978-1-941234-21-1

Copyright © 2014 MG Prep, Inc.

ALL RIGHTS RESERVED. No part of this work may be reproduced or used in any form or by
any means—graphic, electronic, or mechanical, including photocopying, recording, tap-
ing, or web distribution—without the prior written permission of the publisher,
MG Prep, Inc.

Note: *GMAT, Graduate Management Admission Test, Graduate Management Admission
Council,* and *GMAC* are all registered trademarks of the Graduate Management Admission
Council, which neither sponsors nor is affiliated in any way with this product.

Layout Design: Dan McNaney and Cathy Huang
Cover Design: Dan McNaney and Frank Callaghan
Cover Photography: Alli Ugosoli

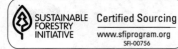

SUSTAINABLE FORESTRY INITIATIVE   Certified Sourcing   www.sfiprogram.org   SFI-00756

INSTRUCTIONAL GUIDE SERIES

0   **GMAT Roadmap**
(ISBN: 978-1-941234-09-9)

1   **Fractions, Decimals, & Percents**
(ISBN: 978-1-941234-02-0)

2   **Algebra**
(ISBN: 978-1-941234-00-6)

3   **Word Problems**
(ISBN: 978-1-941234-08-2)

4   **Geometry**
(ISBN: 978-1-941234-03-7)

5   **Number Properties**
(ISBN: 978-1-941234-05-1)

6   **Critical Reasoning**
(ISBN: 978-1-941234-01-3)

7   **Reading Comprehension**
(ISBN: 978-1-941234-06-8)

8   **Sentence Correction**
(ISBN: 978-1-941234-07-5)

9   **Integrated Reasoning & Essay**
(ISBN: 978-1-941234-04-4)

SUPPLEMENTAL GUIDE SERIES

Math GMAT Supplement Guides

Foundations of GMAT Math
(ISBN: 978-1-935707-59-2)

Advanced GMAT Quant
(ISBN: 978-1-935707-15-8)

Official Guide Companion
(ISBN: 978-0-984178-01-8)

Verbal GMAT Supplement Guides

Foundations of GMAT Verbal
(ISBN: 978-1-935707-01-9)

Official Guide Companion for Sentence Correction
(ISBN: 978-1-937707-41-5)

MANHATTAN
PREP

December 2nd, 2014

Dear Student,

Thank you for picking up a copy of *Algebra*. I hope this book gives you just the guidance you need to get the most out of your GMAT studies.

A great number of people were involved in the creation of the book you are holding. First and foremost is Zeke Vanderhoek, the founder of Manhattan Prep. Zeke was a lone tutor in New York City when he started the company in 2000. Now, well over a decade later, the company contributes to the successes of thousands of students around the globe every year.

Our Manhattan Prep Strategy Guides are based on the continuing experiences of our instructors and students. The overall vision of the 6th Edition GMAT guides was developed by Stacey Koprince, Whitney Garner, and Dave Mahler over the course of many months; Stacey and Dave then led the execution of that vision as the primary author and editor, respectively, of this book. Numerous other instructors made contributions large and small, but I'd like to send particular thanks to Josh Braslow, Kim Cabot, Dmitry Farber, Ron Purewal, Emily Meredith Sledge, and Ryan Starr. Dan McNaney and Cathy Huang provided design and layout expertise as Dan managed book production, while Liz Krisher made sure that all the moving pieces, both inside and outside of our company, came together at just the right time. Finally, we are indebted to all of the Manhattan Prep students who have given us feedback over the years. This book wouldn't be half of what it is without your voice.

At Manhattan Prep, we aspire to provide the best instructors and resources possible, and we hope that you will find our commitment manifest in this book. We strive to keep our books free of errors, but if you think we've goofed, please post to manhattanprep.com/GMAT/errata. If you have any questions or comments in general, please email our Student Services team at gmat@manhattanprep.com. Or give us a shout at 212-721-7400 (or 800-576-4628 in the US or Canada). I look forward to hearing from you.

Thanks again, and best of luck preparing for the GMAT!

Sincerely,

Chris Ryan
Vice President of Academics
Manhattan Prep

HOW TO ACCESS YOUR ONLINE RESOURCES

IF YOU ARE A REGISTERED MANHATTAN PREP STUDENT

and have received this book as part of your course materials, you have AUTOMATIC access to ALL of our online resources. This includes all practice exams, question banks, and online updates to this book. To access these resources, follow the instructions in the Welcome Guide provided to you at the start of your program.
Do NOT follow the instructions below.

IF YOU PURCHASED THIS BOOK FROM MANHATTANPREP.COM OR AT ONE OF OUR CENTERS

1. Go to: **www.manhattanprep.com/gmat/studentcenter**
2. Log in with the username and password you chose when setting up your account.

IF YOU PURCHASED THIS BOOK AT A RETAIL LOCATION

1. Go to: **www.manhattanprep.com/gmat/access**
2. Create an account or, if you already have one, log in on this page with your username and password.
3. Follow the instructions on the screen.

Your one year of online access begins on the day that you register your book at the above URL.

You only need to register your product ONCE at the above URL. To use your online resources any time AFTER you have completed the registration process, log in to the following URL:
www.manhattanprep.com/gmat/studentcenter

Please note that online access is nontransferable. This means that only NEW and UNREGISTERED copies of the book will grant you online access. Previously used books will NOT provide any online resources.

IF YOU PURCHASED AN EBOOK VERSION OF THIS BOOK

1. Create an account with Manhattan Prep at this website:
www.manhattanprep.com/gmat/register
2. Email a copy of your purchase receipt to **gmat@manhattanprep.com** to activate your resources. Please be sure to use the same email address to create an account that you used to purchase the eBook.

For any questions, email **gmat@manhattanprep.com** or call **800-576-4628**.
Please refer to the following page for a description of the online resources that come with this book.

YOUR ONLINE RESOURCES
YOUR PURCHASE INCLUDES ONLINE ACCESS TO THE FOLLOWING:

6 FULL-LENGTH GMAT PRACTICE EXAMS

The 6 full-length GMAT practice exams included with the purchase of this book are delivered online using Manhattan Prep's proprietary computer-adaptive test engine. The exams adapt to your ability level by drawing from a bank of more than 1,200 unique questions of varying difficulty levels written by Manhattan Prep's expert instructors, all of whom have scored in the 99th percentile on the Official GMAT. At the end of each exam you will receive a score, an analysis of your results, and the opportunity to review detailed explanations for each question. You may choose to take the exams timed or untimed.

Important Note: The 6 GMAT exams included with the purchase of this book are the SAME exams that you receive upon purchasing ANY book in the Manhattan Prep GMAT Complete Strategy Guide Set.

5 FREE INTERACT™ LESSONS

Interact™ is a comprehensive self-study program that is fun, intuitive, and directed by you. Each interactive video lesson is taught by an expert Manhattan Prep instructor and includes dozens of individual branching points. The choices you make define the content you see. This book comes with access to the first five lessons of GMAT Interact. Lessons are available on your computer or iPad so you can prep where you are, when you want. For more information on the full version of this program, visit **manhattanprep.com/gmat/interact**

ALGEBRA ONLINE QUESTION BANK

The Online Question Bank for Algebra consists of 25 extra practice questions (with detailed explanations) that test the variety of concepts and skills covered in this book. These questions provide you with extra practice beyond the problem sets contained in this book. You may use our online timer to practice your pacing by setting time limits for each question in the bank.

ONLINE UPDATES TO THE CONTENT IN THIS BOOK

The content presented in this book is updated periodically to ensure that it reflects the GMAT's most current trends. You may view all updates, including any known errors or changes, upon registering for online access.

The above resources can be found in your Student Center at manhattanprep.com/gmat/studentcenter

TABLE *of* CONTENTS

guide **2**

Official Guide Problem Sets

As you work through this strategy guide, it is a very good idea to test your skills using official problems that appeared on the real GMAT in the past. To help you with this step of your studies, we have classified all of the problems from the three main *Official Guide* books and devised some problem sets to accompany this book.

These problem sets live in your Manhattan Prep Student Center so that they can be updated whenever the test makers update their books. When you log into your Student Center, click on the link for the *Official Guide Problem Sets*, found on your home page. Download them today!

The problem sets consist of four broad groups of questions:

1. A mid-term quiz: Take this quiz after completing **Chapter 5** of this guide.

2. A final quiz: Take this quiz after completing this entire guide.

3. A full practice set of questions: If you are taking one of our classes, this is the homework given on your syllabus, so just follow the syllabus assignments. If you are not taking one of our classes, you can do this practice set whenever you feel that you have a very solid understanding of the material taught in this guide.

4. A full reference list of all *Official Guide* problems that test the topics covered in this strategy guide: Use these problems to test yourself on specific topics or to create larger sets of mixed questions.

As you begin studying, try one problem at a time and review it thoroughly before moving on. In the middle of your studies, attempt some mixed sets of problems from a small pool of topics (the two quizzes we've devised for you are good examples of how to do this). Later in your studies, mix topics from multiple guides and include some questions that you've chosen randomly out of the *Official Guide*. This way, you'll learn to be prepared for anything!

Study Tips:

1. DO time yourself when answering questions.

2. DO cut yourself off and make a guess if a question is taking too long. You can try it again later without a time limit, but first practice the behavior you want to exhibit on the real test: let go and move on.

3. DON'T answer all of the *Official Guide* questions by topic or chapter at once. The real test will toss topics at you in random order, and half of the battle is figuring out what each new question is testing. Set yourself up to learn this when doing practice sets.

Chapter *of* 1
Algebra

PEMDAS

In This Chapter...

Chapter 1
PEMDAS

When simplifying an algebraic expression, you have to follow a specific order of operations. The correct order of operations is: Parentheses-Exponents-(Multiplication/Division)-(Addition/Subtraction), or PEMDAS in the United States. If you learned math in other English-speaking countries, you may have memorized slightly different acronyms; the rules are still the same. Multiplication and division are in parentheses because they are on the *same* level of priority. The same is true of addition and subtraction. When two or more operations are at the same level of priority, always work from left to right.

$$\text{Simplify } 5 + (2 \times 4 + 2)^2 - |7(-4)| + 18 \div 3 \times 5 - 8.$$

P = PARENTHESES. First, perform all of the operations that are *inside* parentheses. Note that in terms of order of operations, absolute value signs are equivalent to parentheses. In this expression, there are two groups of parentheses:

$(2 \times 4 + 2)$ and $|7(-4)|$

In the first group, there are two operations to perform, multiplication and addition. According to PEMDAS, multiplication must come before addition:

$(2 \times 4 + 2) = (8 + 2) = 10$

In the second group, perform the operation inside first (multiplication), then take the absolute value of that number:

$|7(-4)| = |-28| = 28$

Now the original expression looks like this:

$5 + 10^2 - 28 + 18 \div 3 \times 5 - 8$

E = EXPONENTS. Second, take care of any exponents in the expression:

$10^2 = 100$

Now the expression looks like this:

$5 + 100 - 28 + 18 \div 3 \times 5 - 8$

M&D = MULTIPLICATION & DIVISION. Next, perform all the multiplication and division. Work from left to right:

$$18 \div 3 \times 5$$
$$6 \quad \times 5 = 30$$

Now the expression reads:

$$5 + 100 - 28 + 30 - 8$$

A&S = ADDITION & SUBTRACTION. Lastly, perform all the addition and subtraction. Work from left to right.

$$5 + 100 - 28 + 30 - 8$$
$$105 - 28 + 30 - 8$$
$$77 + 30 - 8$$
$$107 - 8$$

The answer: **99**

Subtraction of Expressions

One of the most common errors involving the order of operations occurs when an expression with multiple terms is subtracted. The subtraction must occur across *every* term within the expression. Each term in the subtracted part must have its sign reversed. For example:

$$x - (y - z) = x - y + z$$ (Note that the signs of both y and $-z$ have been reversed.)

$$x - (y + z) = x - y - z$$ (Note that the signs of both y and z have been reversed.)

$$x - 2(y - 3z) = x - 2y + 6z$$ (Note that the signs of both y and $-3z$ have been reversed.)

Now try another example:

What is $5x - [y - (3x - 4y)]$?

Both expressions in parentheses must be subtracted, so the signs of each term must be reversed for *each* subtraction. Note that the square brackets are just fancy parentheses, used so that you avoid having parentheses right next to each other.

$$5x - [y - (3x - 4y)] =$$
$$5x - (y - 3x + 4y) =$$
$$5x - (5y - 3x) =$$
$$5x - 5y + 3x = \mathbf{8x - 5y}$$

Fraction Bars as Grouping Symbols

Even though fraction bars do not fit into the PEMDAS hierarchy, they do take precedence. In any expression with a fraction bar, pretend that there are parentheses around the numerator and denominator of the fraction. This may be obvious as long as the fraction bar remains in the expression, but it is easy to forget if you eliminate the fraction bar or add or subtract fractions. For example:

Simplify: $\dfrac{x-1}{2} - \dfrac{2x-1}{3}$

The common denominator for the two fractions is 6, so multiply the numerator and denominator of the first fraction by 3, and those of the second fraction by 2:

$$\frac{x-1}{2}\left(\frac{3}{3}\right) - \frac{2x-1}{3}\left(\frac{2}{2}\right) = \frac{3x-3}{6} - \frac{4x-2}{6}$$

Treat the expressions $3x - 3$ and $4x - 2$ as though they were enclosed in parentheses! Accordingly, once you make the common denominator, actually put in parentheses for these numerators. Then reverse the signs of both terms in the second numerator:

$$\frac{(3x-3)-(4x-2)}{6} = \frac{3x-3-4x+2}{6} = \frac{-x-1}{6} = -\frac{x+1}{6}$$

Problem Set

1. Evaluate: $(4 + 12 \div 3 - 18) - [-11 - (-4)]$

2. Evaluate: $-|-13 - (-17)|$

3. Evaluate: $\left(\dfrac{4+8}{2-(-6)} \right) - (4 + 8 \div 2 - (-6))$

4. Simplify: $x - (3 - x)$

5. Simplify: $(4 - y) - 2(2y - 3)$

Solutions

1. **−3:** $(4 + 12 \div 3 - 18) - (-11 - (-4)) =$

$\qquad\qquad (4 + 4 - 18) - (-11 + 4) =$ Division before addition/subtraction

$\qquad\qquad\qquad (-10) - (-7) =$ Subtraction of negative = addition

$\qquad\qquad\qquad\qquad -10 + 7 = -3$ Arithmetic—watch the signs!

2. **−4:** $-|-13 - (-17)| =$

$\qquad\qquad -|-13 + 17)| =$ Subtraction of negative = addition

$\qquad\qquad\qquad -|4| = -4$

Note that the absolute value *cannot* be made into 13 + 17. You must perform the arithmetic inside grouping symbols *first*, whether inside parentheses or inside absolute value bars. *Then* you can remove the grouping symbols.

3. $-\dfrac{25}{2}$ **or** $-12\dfrac{1}{2}$: $\left[\dfrac{4+8}{\underbrace{2-(-6)}}\right] - [4 + 8 \div 2 - (-6)] =$

$$\left(\dfrac{4+8}{\underbrace{2+6}}\right) - (4 + 8 \div 2 + 6) =$$

$$\left(\dfrac{12}{8}\right) - \left(\underbrace{4 + 4 + 6}\right) =$$

$$\dfrac{3}{2} - 14 =$$

$$\dfrac{3}{2} - \dfrac{28}{2} = -\dfrac{25}{2} \text{ or } -12\dfrac{1}{2}$$

4. $2x - 3$**:** Do not forget to reverse the signs of every term in a subtracted expression:

$\qquad x - (3 - x) = x - 3 + x = 2x - 3$

5. **−5y + 10 (or 10 − 5y):** Do not forget to reverse the signs of every term in a subtracted expression:

$\qquad (4 - y) - 2(2y - 3) = 4 - y - 4y + 6 = -5y + 10 \text{ (or } 10 - 5y)$

Chapter 2
of

Algebra

Linear Equations

In This Chapter. . .

Chapter 2

Linear Equations

Linear equations are equations in which all variables have an exponent of 1. For example, the equation $x - 13 = 24$ is linear because the variable x is raised to the first power.

Expressions vs. Equations

The most basic difference between expressions and equations is that equations contain an equals sign, and expressions do not.

An expression, even one that contains variables, represents a value. When manipulating or simplifying expressions, you have to follow certain rules to ensure that you don't change the value of the expression.

There are several methods for simplifying expressions. You can:

1. Combine like terms $\qquad\qquad\qquad 6z + 5z \rightarrow 11z$

2. Find a common denominator $\qquad \dfrac{1}{12} + \dfrac{3x^3}{4} \times \left(\dfrac{3}{3}\right) \rightarrow \dfrac{1}{12} + \dfrac{9x^3}{12} = \dfrac{9x^3 + 1}{12}$

3. Pull out a common factor $\qquad 2ab + 4b \rightarrow 2b(a + 2)$

4. Cancel common factors $\qquad\qquad \dfrac{5y^3}{25y} \rightarrow \dfrac{y^2}{5}$

What all of these moves have in common is that the value of the expression stays the same. If you plug numbers into the original and simplified forms, the value is the same. For example, replace z in the first expression with 3:

$6z + 5z$	$11z$
$6(3) + 5(3)$	$11(3)$
$18 + 15$	33
33	

Thus, $6z + 5z$ is equivalent to $11z$.

Equations behave differently. An equation contains an equals sign. In order to keep the two sides of the equation equal, any change you make to one side must also be made to the other side. Also, while the two sides are still equal, the change may alter the values on both sides of the equation.

$3 = 3$	An equivalence
$2 \times (3) = (3) \times 2$	Multiply both sides by 2
$6 = 6$	The two sides are still equal, but have different values

In general, there are six operations you can perform to both sides of an equation. Remember to perform the action on the *entire* side of the equation. For example, if you were to square both sides of the equation $\sqrt{x} + 1 = x$, you would have to square the entire expression $(\sqrt{x} + 1)$, as opposed to squaring each term individually.

You can:

1. Add the same thing to both sides

$$z - 13 = -14$$
$$\underline{+13 \quad +13}$$
$$z \quad\quad = -1$$

2. Subtract the same thing from both sides

$$x + 8 = 34$$
$$\underline{-8 \quad -8}$$
$$x \quad\quad = 26$$

3. Multiply both sides by the same thing

$$\frac{4}{a} = a + b$$
$$a \times \left(\frac{4}{a}\right) = (a + b) \times a$$
$$4 = a^2 + ab$$

4. Divide both sides by the same thing

$$3x = 6y + 12$$
$$\frac{3x}{3} = \frac{6y + 12}{3}$$
$$x = 2y + 4$$

MANHATTAN
PREP

5. Raise both sides to the same power

$$\sqrt{y} = y + 2$$
$$\left(\sqrt{y}\right)^2 = (y+2)^2$$
$$y = (y+2)^2$$

6. Take the same root of both sides

$$x^3 = 125$$
$$\sqrt[3]{x^3} = \sqrt[3]{125}$$
$$x = 5$$

2

Solving One-Variable Equations

In order to solve one-variable equations, isolate the variable on one side of the equation. In doing so, make sure you perform identical operations to both sides of the equation. Here are three examples:

$3x + 5 = 26$	Subtract 5 from both sides.
$3x = 21$	Divide both sides by 3.
$x = 7$	

$w = 17w - 1$	Subtract w from both sides.
$0 = 16w - 1$	Add 1 to both sides.
$1 = 16w$	Divide both sides by 16.
$\dfrac{1}{16} = w$	

$\dfrac{p}{9} + 3 = 5$	Subtract 3 from both sides.
$\dfrac{p}{9} = 2$	Multiply both sides by 9.
$p = 18$	

Simultaneous Equations: Solving by Substitution

Sometimes the GMAT asks you to solve a system of equations with more than one variable. You might be given two equations with two variables, or perhaps three equations with three variables. In either case, there are two primary ways of solving simultaneous equations: by substitution or by combination.

Use substitution to solve the following for x and y.

$$x + y = 9$$
$$2x = 5y + 4$$

First, solve the first equation for x.

$$x + y = 9$$
$$x = 9 - y$$

Next, substitute the expression $9 - y$ into the second equation wherever x appears.

$$2x = 5y + 4$$
$$2(9 - y) = 5y + 4$$

Then, solve the second equation for y. You will now get a number for y.

$$2(9 - y) = 5y + 4$$
$$18 - 2y = 5y + 4$$
$$14 = 7y$$
$$2 = y$$

Finally, substitute your solution for y into either of the original equations in order to solve for x.

$$x + y = 9$$
$$x + 2 = 9$$
$$x = 7$$

You could also have started this process by solving the first equation for y and then substituting the expression $9 - x$ in place of y in the second equation.

Simultaneous Equations: Solving by Combination

Alternatively, you can solve simultaneous equations by combination. In this method, add or subtract the two equations to eliminate one of the variables.

Solve the following for x and y.

$$x + y = 9$$
$$2x = 5y + 4$$

To start, line up the terms of the equations.

$$x \ + y = 9$$
$$2x - 5y = 4$$

The goal is to make one of two things happen: either the coefficient in front of one of the variables (say, x) is the same in both equations, in which case you subtract one equation from the other, or the coefficient in front of one of the variables is the same but with opposite signs, in which case you add the two equations. You do this by multiplying one of the equations by some number. For example, multiply the first equation by -2:

$$-2(x + y = 9) \quad \rightarrow \quad -2x - 2y = -18$$
$$2x - 5y = 4 \quad \rightarrow \quad 2x - 5y = 4$$

Next, add the equations to eliminate one of the variables.

$$\begin{array}{r} -2x - 2y = -18 \\ +\quad 2x - 5y = 4 \\ \hline -7y = -14 \end{array}$$

Now, solve the resulting equation for the unknown variable.

$$-7y = -14$$
$$y = 2$$

Finally, substitute into one of the original equations to solve for the second variable.

$$x + y = 9$$
$$x + 2 = 9$$
$$x = 7$$

Absolute Value Equations

Absolute value refers to the *positive* value of the expression within the absolute value brackets. Equations that involve absolute value generally have two solutions. In other words, there are *two* numbers that the variable could equal in order to make the equation true, because the value of the expression inside the absolute value brackets could be *positive or negative*. For instance, if you know $|x| = 5$, then x could be either 5 or −5 and the equation would still be true.

Use the following two-step method when solving for a variable expression inside absolute value brackets.

> Solve for *w*, given that $12 + |w - 4| = 30$.

Step 1: Isolate the expression within the absolute value brackets.

$$12 + |w - 4| = 30$$
$$|w - 4| = 18$$

Step 2: Once you have an equation of the form $|x| = a$ with $a > 0$, you know that $x = \pm a$. Remove the absolute value brackets and solve the equation for two different cases:

CASE 1: $x = a$ (*x* is positive)   CASE 2: $x = -a$ (*x* is negative)
$$w - 4 = 18 \qquad\qquad\qquad w - 4 = -18$$
$$w = 22 \qquad\qquad\qquad\quad w = -14$$

Problem Set

Now that you've finished the chapter, do the following problems.

1.   Solve for x: $2(2 - 3x) - (4 + x) = 7$

2.   Solve for z: $\dfrac{4z - 7}{3 - 2z} = -5$

3.   Solve for y: $22 - |y + 14| = 20$

4.   Solve for x and y: $y = 2x + 9$ and $7x + 3y = -51$

Save the below problem set for review, either after you finish this book or after you finish all of the Quant books that you plan to study.

5.   Every attendee at a monster truck rally paid the same admission fee. How many people attended the rally?

    (1)   If the admission fee had been raised to \$20 and twice as many people had attended, the total admission fees collected would have been three times greater.

    (2)   If the admission fee had been raised to \$30 and two-thirds as many people had attended, the total admission fees collected would have been 150% of the actual admission fees collected.

6.   Solve for x: $x\left(x - \dfrac{5x + 6}{x}\right) = 0$

7.   Solve for x: $\dfrac{3x - 6}{5} = x - 6$

8.   Solve for x: $\dfrac{x + 2}{4 + x} = \dfrac{5}{9}$

Solutions

1. −1:

$$2(2 - 3x) - (4 + x) = 7$$
$$4 - 6x - 4 - x = 7$$
$$-7x = 7$$
$$x = -1$$

2. $\dfrac{4}{3}$:

$$\frac{4z - 7}{3 - 2z} = -5$$
$$4z - 7 = -5(3 - 2z)$$
$$4z - 7 = -15 + 10z$$
$$8 = 6z$$
$$z = \frac{8}{6} = \frac{4}{3}$$

3. $y = \{-16, -12\}$: First, isolate the expression within the absolute value brackets. Then, solve for two cases, one in which the expression is positive and one in which it is negative:

$$22 - |y + 14| = 20$$
$$2 = |y + 14|$$

Case 1: $y + 14 = 2$ Case 2: $y + 14 = -2$
$\qquad\quad y = -12$ $y = -16$

4. $x = -6$; $y = -3$: Solve this system by substitution. Substitute the value given for y in the first equation into the second equation. Then, distribute, combine like terms, and solve. Once you get a value for x, substitute it back into the first equation to obtain the value of y:

$$y = 2x + 9 \qquad 7x + 3y = -51$$
$$7x + 3(2x + 9) = -51$$
$$7x + 6x + 27 = -51$$
$$13x + 27 = -51$$
$$13x = -78$$
$$x = -6$$

$$y = 2x + 9 = 2(-6) + 9 = -3$$

5. (E): This question asks how many people attended a monster truck rally. The number of attendees times the admission fee equals the total amount collected, as such:

Total = Attendees × Price
$$T = A \times P$$

You want to know A.

(1) INSUFFICIENT: If the price had been $20 and twice as many people had attended, the total would be three times greater. Therefore:

$$3T = 2A \times 20$$
$$3T = 40A$$

This is not sufficient to solve for A.

(2) INSUFFICIENT: If the price had been $30 and two-thirds as many people had attended, the total would be 150% of the actual total. Therefore:

$$1.5T = \frac{2}{3}A \times 30$$
$$1.5T = 20A$$

This is not sufficient to solve for A.

(1) AND (2) INSUFFICIENT: Don't fall for the trap that two equations for two variables is enough to solve. Notice that $3T = 40A$ and $1.5T = 20A$ are identical. Combining the two statements is therefore no more sufficient than either statement alone.

The correct answer is (E).

6. **{6, −1}:** Distribute the multiplication by x. Note that, when you cancel the x in the denominator, the quantity $5x + 6$ is implicitly enclosed in parentheses!

$$x\left(x - \frac{5x+6}{x}\right) = 0$$
$$x^2 - (5x + 6) = 0$$
$$x^2 - 5x - 6 = 0$$
$$(x - 6)(x + 1) = 0$$
$$x = 6 \text{ or } -1$$

Note also that the value 0 is impossible for x, because x is in a denominator by itself in the original equation. You are not allowed to divide by 0. Do not look at the product in the original equation and deduce that $x = 0$ is a solution.

7. **12:** Solve by multiplying both sides by 5 to eliminate the denominator. Then, distribute and isolate the variable:

$$\frac{3x-6}{5} = x - 6$$
$$3x - 6 = 5(x - 6)$$
$$3x - 6 = 5x - 30$$
$$24 = 2x$$
$$12 = x$$

MANHATTAN
PREP

8. $x = \dfrac{1}{2}$: Cross-multiply to eliminate the denominators. Then, distribute and solve:

$$\frac{x+2}{4+x} = \frac{5}{9}$$

$$9(x + 2) = 5(4 + x)$$

$$9x + 18 = 20 + 5x$$

$$4x = 2$$

$$x = \frac{1}{2}$$

2

Chapter 3 *of* Algebra

Strategy: Choose Smart Numbers

In This Chapter...

Chapter 3

Strategy: Choose Smart Numbers

Some algebra problems—problems that involve unknowns, or variables—can be turned into arithmetic problems instead. You're better at arithmetic than algebra (everybody is!), so turning an annoying variable-based problem into one that uses real numbers can save time and aggravation on the GMAT.

Which of the below two problems is easier for you to solve?

If *n* employees are fulfilling orders at the rate of 3 orders per employee per hour, how many orders are filled in 4 hours?	If 2 employees are fulfilling orders at the rate of 3 orders per employee per hour, how many orders are filled in 4 hours?
(A) 3*n* (B) 4*n* (C) 12*n*	(A) 6 (B) 12 (C) 24

In the first problem, you would write an expression using the variable *n* and then you would use algebra to solve. You may think that this version is not particularly difficult, but no matter how easy you think it is, it's still easier to work with real numbers.

The set-up of the two problems is identical—and this feature is at the heart of how you can turn algebra into arithmetic.

How Do Smart Numbers Work?

Here's how to solve the algebra version of the above problem using smart numbers.

Step 1: *Choose smart numbers* to replace the unknowns.

How do you know you can choose a random number in the first place? The problem talks about a number but only supplies a variable for that number. It never supplies a real value for that number anywhere in the problem or in the answers.

Instead, choose a real number. In general, 2 is a often a good number to choose on algebraic smart number problems.

Step 2: *Solve* the problem using your chosen smart numbers.

Wherever the problem talks about the *number*, it now says 2:

> If 2 employees are fulfilling orders at the rate of 3 orders per employee per hour, how many orders are filled in 4 hours?

Do the math! If 2 employees fulfill 3 orders per hour, then together they fulfill 6 orders per hour. In 4 hours, they'll fulfill 24 orders.

Step 3: *Find a match* in the answers. Plug $n = 2$ into the answers.

    (A) $3n = (3)(2) = 6$
    (B) $4n = (4)(2) = 8$
    (C) $12n = (12)(2) = 24$

The correct answer is **(C)**.

Keep an eye out for problems that contain variable expressions (no equations or inequality signs) in the answers; many of these problems can be solved by choosing smart numbers.

When to Choose Smart Numbers

It's crucial to know when you're allowed to use this technique. It's also crucial to know how *you* are going to decide whether to use textbook math or choose smart numbers; you will typically have time to try just one of the two techniques during your two minutes on the problem.

The *Choose Smart Numbers* technique can be used any time a problem contains only *unspecified* values. The easiest example of such a problem is one that contains variables, percents, fractions, or ratios throughout. It does not provide real numbers for those variables, even in the answer choices. Whenever a problem has this characteristic, you can choose your own smart numbers to turn the problem into arithmetic.

There is some cost to doing so: it can take extra time compared to the "pure" textbook solution. As a result, the technique is most useful when the problem is a hard one for you. If you find the algebra involved to be very easy, then you may not want to take the time to transform the problem into arithmetic. As the math gets more complicated, however, the arithmetic form becomes comparatively easier and faster to use.

Try this problem. Solve it twice; once using textbook math and once using smart numbers:

> A store bought a box of 50 t-shirts for a total of x dollars. The store then sold each t-shirt for a premium of 25% over the original cost per shirt. In terms of x, how much did the store charge for each shirt?

(A) $\dfrac{x}{4}$

(B) $\dfrac{5x}{4}$

(C) $\dfrac{x}{40}$

(D) $125x$

(E) $\dfrac{125}{x}$

First, how do you know that you can choose smart numbers on this problem? The problem talks about the price of a box of t-shirts but never mentions a real number for that price anywhere along the way.

Step 1: Choose smart numbers.

Make your life easy and choose a number that will work nicely in the problem. What is the first math operation you'll need to do?

You need the cost per t-shirt, so you'll have to divide x by 50. Pick a number, then, that is not already in the problem (so don't use 50 itself) but that will divide evenly by 50. The number 100 is the smallest number that fits the bill.

Step 2: Solve.

The store paid $100 for the box of 50 t-shirts, or $2 per t-shirt.

The store then charged a 25% premium. Take 25% of $2 and add it to the total:

$$\$2 + (0.25)(\$2) = \$2 + \$0.50 = \$2.50$$

The store sold the t-shirts for $2.50 each.

Step 3: Find a match.

Plug $x = 100$ into the answers. At any point that you can tell that a particular answer will not equal $2.50, stop and cross off that answer.

(A) $\dfrac{x}{4} = \dfrac{100}{4} = 25$

(B) $\dfrac{5x}{4} = \dfrac{5(100)}{4} = $ too big

(C) $\dfrac{x}{40} = \dfrac{100}{40} = \dfrac{10}{4} = 2.5$ Match!

(D) $125x = 125(100) = $ too big

(E) $\dfrac{125}{x} = \dfrac{125}{100} = 1.25$

The correct answer is **(C)**.

Here's the algebraic solution:

The store bought 50 t-shirts for a total of x dollars, or $\dfrac{x}{50}$ dollars per shirt. The store then sold the shirts for a 25% premium over that original cost. Set up an equation to solve:

Sale price per shirt = (Cost per shirt) + (Premium applied to cost)

$$S = \dfrac{x}{50} + (0.25)\left(\dfrac{x}{50}\right)$$

$$(1.25)\, S = \dfrac{x}{50} = \left(\dfrac{x}{50}\right)\left(\dfrac{5}{4}\right) = \left(\dfrac{x}{10}\right)\left(\dfrac{1}{4}\right) = \dfrac{x}{40}$$

The correct answer is **(C)**. That may seem like less work, but take a look at some of the wrong answers:

(B) $\dfrac{5x}{4}$ Mistake: assume x is cost per shirt, instead of $\dfrac{x}{50}$.

(D) $125x$ Mistake: assume x is cost per shirt *and* multiply by 125 instead of 125%.

Answers (A) and (E) also involve mixing up legitimate calculations.

As a general rule, if you find the algebra easy, go ahead and solve that way. When the algebra becomes hard for you, though, then switch to smart numbers. If you realize you made a careless mistake with the algebra, that may be a signal that you should have used smart numbers instead.

MANHATTAN
PREP

How to Pick Good Numbers

Half of the battle lies in learning how to choose numbers that work well with the given problem. Try this one:

> A truck can carry x shipping containers and each container can hold y gallons of milk. If one truck is filled to capacity and a second one is half full, how many gallons of milk are they carrying, in terms of x and y?
>
> (A) $x + 0.5y$
> (B) $x + y$
> (C) $0.5xy$
> (D) $1.5xy$
> (E) $2xy$

Step 1: Choose smart numbers.

Try $x = 1$ and $y = 2$.

Step 2: Solve.

Each truck has one shipping container. The first truck is filled to capacity, so it carries 2 gallons of milk. The second is half full, so it carries 1 gallon. Together, the trucks carry 3 gallons of milk.

Step 3: Find a match.

    (A) $x + 0.5y = 1 + (0.5)(2) = 2$
    (B) $x + y = 1 + 2 = 3$ Match!
    (C) $0.5xy = (0.5)(1)(2) = 1$
    (D) $1.5xy = (1.5)(1)(2) = 3$ Wait a second—this one matches too!
    (E) $2xy = 2(1)(2) = 4$

In rare circumstances, the number you choose could work for more than one answer choice. Now what? While the clock is still ticking, either guess between (B) and (D) or, if you have time, try a different set of numbers in the problem.

Afterwards, learn a valuable lesson about how to choose the best smart numbers: if you choose 0 or 1, you increase the chances that more than one answer will work, because those two numbers both have strange properties.

Try $x = 2$ and $y = 3$ instead. The first truck is carrying $(2)(3) = 6$ gallons of milk. The second carries half that, or 3 gallons. Together, they carry 9 gallons of milk.

You've already eliminated answers (A), (C), and (E), so you only need to try (B) and (D):

(B) $x + y = 2 + 3 = 5$ Not a match
(D) $1.5xy = (1.5)(2)(3) = 9$ Match!

The correct answer is **(D)**.

If you follow the guidelines below for choosing numbers, then the above situation is much less likely to occur:

- Do not pick 0 or 1.

- Do not pick numbers that appear elsewhere in the problem.

- If you have to choose multiple numbers, choose different numbers, ideally with different properties (e.g., odd and even). The second case above used one odd and one even number, just in case.

If you do accidentally find yourself in this situation and you have the time, then go back, change one of the numbers in your problem, and do the math again. If you don't have time, just pick one of the two answers that did work.

Here's a summary of the Choose Smart Numbers strategy:

Step 0: Recognize that you can choose smart numbers.

The problem talks about some values but doesn't provide real numbers for those values. Rather, it uses variables or only refers to fractions or percents. The answer choices consist of variable expressions, fractions, or percents. (See the *Fractions, Decimals, & Percents GMAT Strategy Guide* for more on using smart numbers.)

Step 1: Choose smart numbers.

1. If you have to pick for more than one variable, pick different numbers for each one. If possible, pick numbers with different characteristics (e.g., one even and one odd).

2. Follow any constraints given in the problem. You may be restricted to positive numbers or to integers, for example, depending upon the way the problem is worded.

3. Avoid choosing 0, 1, or numbers that already appear in the problem.

4. Choose numbers that work easily in the problem. The numbers 2, 3, and 5 are often good numbers to use for algebra problems. If you have to divide, try to pick a number that will yield an integer after the division.

Step 2: Solve the problem using your chosen smart numbers.

Wherever the problem used to have variables or unknowns, it now contains the real numbers that you've chosen. Solve the problem arithmetically and find your target answer.

Step 3: Find a match in the answers.

Plug your smart numbers into the variables in the answer choices and look for the choice that matches your target. If, at any point, you can tell that a particular answer will *not* match your target, stop calculating that answer. Cross it off and move on to the next answer.

How to Get Better at Smart Numbers

Practice makes perfect! First, try the problem sets associated with this book. When you think smart numbers can be used, try each problem two times: once using smart numbers and once using the "textbook" method. (Time yourself separately for each attempt.)

When you're done, ask yourself which way you prefer to solve *this* problem and why. On the real test, you won't have time to try both methods; you'll have to make a decision and go with it. Learn *how* to make that decision while studying; then, the next time a new problem pops up in front of you that could be solved by choosing smart numbers, you'll be able to make a quick (and good!) decision.

Keep an eye out for other opportunities to choose smart numbers throughout the rest of this guide, as well as other guides. This strategy is very useful!

Finally, one important note: at first, you may find yourself always choosing the textbook approach. You've practiced algebra for years, after all, and you've only been using the choose smart numbers technique for a short period of time. Keep practicing; you'll get better! Every high scorer on the Quant section will tell you that choosing smart numbers is invaluable to getting through Quant on time and with a consistent enough performance to reach a top score.

When NOT to Use Smart Numbers

There are certain scenarios in which a problem contains some of the smart numbers characteristics but not all. For example, why can't you use smart numbers on this problem?

> Four brothers split a sum of money between them. The first brother received 50% of the total, the second received 25% of the total, the third received 20% of the total, and the fourth received the remaining $4. How many dollars did the four brothers split?
>
> (A)   50
> (B)   60
> (C)   75
> (D)   80
> (E)   100

The problem talks about a sum of money but, at first, tells you nothing concrete about this sum of money. Towards the end, though, it does give you one real value: $4. Because the "remaining" percent has to equal $4 exactly, this problem has just one numerical answer. You can't pick any starting point that you want. (The answer to the above problem is (D), by the way!)

Problem Set

1. Seamus has 3 times as many marbles as Ronit, and Taj has 7 times as many marbles as Ronit. If Seamus has s marbles then, in terms of s, how many marbles do Seamus, Ronit, and Taj have together?

    (A) $\dfrac{3}{7}s$

    (B) $\dfrac{7}{3}s$

    (C) $\dfrac{11}{3}s$

    (D) $7s$

    (E) $11s$

2. If $x = a + b$ and $y = a + 2b$, then what is $a - b$, in terms of x and y ?

    (A) $2y - 3x$
    (B) $3y - 2x$
    (C) $2x - 3y$
    (D) $2x + 3y$
    (E) $3x - 2y$

3. Cost is expressed by the formula tb^4. If b is doubled and t remains the same, the new cost is how many times greater than the original cost?

    (A) 1.2
    (B) 2
    (C) 6
    (D) 8
    (E) 16

Solutions

1. **(C):** The problem will be easier to solve if you can choose numbers that will give you all integers as you solve. Both Seamus and Taj have a multiple of the number of marbles that Ronit has, so begin by picking for Ronit, not for Seamus.

If Ronit has 2 marbles, then Seamus has (3)(2) = 6 marbles and Taj has (7)(2) = 14 marbles. Together, the three have 22 marbles.

Plug $s = 6$ into the answers (remember that the problem asks about Seamus's starting number, not Ronit's!) and look for a match of 22:

(A) $\dfrac{3}{7}s$ = not an integer

(B) $\dfrac{7}{3}s = \dfrac{7}{3}(6) = 14$. Not a match.

(C) $\dfrac{11}{3}s = \dfrac{11}{3}(6) = 22$. Match!

(D) $7s = 42$. Not a match.

(E) $11s$ = Too large.

Alternatively, you can use an algebraic approach. Begin by translating the first sentence into equations:

$$s = 3r$$
$$t = 7r$$

The question asks for the sum of the three:

$$s + r + t = ?$$

The answers use only s, so figure out how to substitute to leave only s in the equation:

$$r = \frac{s}{3}$$
$$t = 7r = 7\left(\frac{s}{3}\right)$$

Substitute those into the question:

$$s + r + t$$

$$s + \frac{s}{3} + 7\left(\frac{s}{3}\right)$$

$$\frac{3s}{3} + \frac{s}{3} + \frac{7s}{3}$$

$$\frac{11s}{3}$$

3

The correct answer is **(C)**.

2. **(E):** With so many variables, choosing smart numbers will probably be more efficient. Because x and y can be found by certain sums of a and b, pick for a and b, then calculate x and y.

If $a = 5$ and $b = 2$, then $x = 5 + 2 = 7$ and $y = 5 + 2(2) = 9$. The difference $a - b = 5 - 2 = 3$.

Plug $x = 7$ and $y = 9$ into the answers and look for a match of 3:

(A) $2y - 3x = 2(9) - 3(7) = 18 - 21 = $ negative

(B) $3y - 2x = 3(9) - 2(7) = 27 - 14 = 13$

(C) $2x - 3y = 2(7) - 3(9) = 14 - 27 = $ negative

(D) $2x + 3y = 2(7) + 3(9) = $ too big

(E) $3x - 2y = 3(7) - 2(9) = 21 - 18 = 3$. Match!

You can also use an algebraic approach.

>Given: $x = a + b$
>Given: $y = a + 2b$
>What is $a - b$?

The answers use only x and y, so figure out how to rewrite the given equations to plug into the question, using only x and y.

If you subtract the two equations, you'll get x and y in terms of b alone:

$$\begin{array}{r} y = a + 2b \\ \underline{-(x = a + b)} \\ y - x = b \end{array}$$

Multiply the $x = a + b$ equation by 2 and perform the same operation to get x and y in terms of a alone:

$$2x = 2a + 2b$$
$$\underline{-(y = a + 2b)}$$
$$2x - y = a$$

Then, find $a - b$:

$$(2x - y) - (y - x)$$
$$2x - y - y + x$$
$$3x - 2y$$

The correct answer is **(E)**.

3. (E): The problem gives the formula $C = tb^4$ but never offers a real number for the cost or for any of the other variables in the problem. Choose your own smart numbers!

First, use your numbers to find the original cost. Then, double the value of b and find the new cost. Finally divide the new cost by the original cost to determine how many times greater it is.

If, for the *original* cost, $b = 2$ and $t = 3$, then the original cost was $(3)(2^4) = (3)(16)$. Don't multiply that out—remember that you're going to divide later and t doesn't change, so you'll be able to cross 3 off later.

For the new cost, $b = 4$ and $t = 3$, so the cost is $(3)(4^4) = (3)(4^4)$:

$$\frac{\text{new cost}}{\text{original cost}} = \frac{(3)(4^4)}{(3)(2^4)}$$

Simplify before you multiply. The 3s cancel out. Write out the remaining terms:

$$\frac{(4 \times 4 \times 4 \times 4)}{(2 \times 2 \times 2 \times 2)}$$

All of the 2's on the bottom cancel out two of the 4's on top, leaving you with $(4)(4) = 16$.

Alternatively, use an algebraic approach.

$$\text{Original cost} = tb^4$$
$$\text{New cost} = t(2b)^4 = 16tb^4$$

$$\frac{\text{new cost}}{\text{original cost}} = \frac{16tb^4}{tb^4} = 16$$

The correct answer is **(E)**.

Chapter 4

of Algebra

Exponents

In This Chapter...

Chapter 4

Exponents

The mathematical expression 4^3 consists of a base (4) and an exponent (3).

The base (4) is multiplied by itself as many times as the power requires (3):

$$4^3 = 4 \times 4 \times 4 = 64$$

In other words, exponents are actually shorthand for repeated multiplication.

Two exponents have special names: the exponent 2 is called the square, and the exponent 3 is called the cube:

5^2 can be read as five squared ($5^2 = 5 \times 5 = 25$).
5^3 can be read as five cubed ($5^3 = 5 \times 5 \times 5 = 125$).

All About the Base

A Variable Base

Variables can also be raised to an exponent, and they behave the same as numbers:

$$y^4 = y \times y \times y \times y$$

<u>Base of 0 or 1</u>

0 raised to *any* power equals 0.
1 raised to *any* power equals 1.

For example, $0^3 = 0 \times 0 \times 0 = 0$ and $0^4 = 0 \times 0 \times 0 \times 0 = 0$.

Similarly, $1^3 = 1 \times 1 \times 1 = 1$ and $1^4 = 1 \times 1 \times 1 \times 1 = 1$.

If you are told that $x = x^2$, then x must be either 0 or 1.

A Fractional Base

When the base of an exponential expression is a positive proper fraction (in other words, a fraction between 0 and 1), an interesting thing occurs: as the exponent increases, the value of the expression decreases! For example:

$$\left(\frac{3}{4}\right)^1 = \frac{3}{4} \qquad\qquad \left(\frac{3}{4}\right)^2 = \frac{3}{4} \times \frac{3}{4} = \frac{9}{16} \qquad\qquad \left(\frac{3}{4}\right)^3 = \frac{3}{4} \times \frac{3}{4} \times \frac{3}{4} = \frac{27}{64}$$

Notice that $\frac{3}{4} > \frac{9}{16} > \frac{27}{64}$. Positive fractions get smaller, not larger, when raised to higher powers.

You could also distribute the exponent before multiplying. For example:

$$\left(\frac{3}{4}\right)^1 = \frac{3^1}{4^1} = \frac{3}{4} \qquad\qquad \left(\frac{3}{4}\right)^2 = \frac{3^2}{4^2} = \frac{9}{16} \qquad\qquad \left(\frac{3}{4}\right)^3 = \frac{3^3}{4^3} = \frac{27}{64}$$

Note that, just like proper fractions, decimals between 0 and 1 decrease as their exponent increases:

$$(0.6)^2 = 0.36 \qquad\qquad (0.5)^4 = 0.0625 \qquad\qquad (0.1)^5 = 0.00001$$

A Compound Base

Just as an exponent can be distributed to a fraction, it can also be distributed to a product:

$$10^3 = (2 \times 5)^3 = (2)^3 \times (5)^3 = 8 \times 125 = 1{,}000$$

This also works if the base includes variables:

$$(3x)^4 = 3^4 \times x^4 = 81x^4$$

A Base of −1

$$(-1)^1 = -1 \qquad (-1)^2 = -1 \times -1 = 1 \qquad (-1)^3 = -1 \times -1 \times -1 = -1$$

This pattern repeats indefinitely. In general:

$$(-1)^{\text{ODD}} = -1 \qquad\qquad (-1)^{\text{EVEN}} = 1$$

A Negative Base

When dealing with negative bases, pay particular attention to PEMDAS. Unless the negative sign is inside parentheses, the exponent does not distribute. For example:

$$-2^4 \qquad\qquad \neq \qquad\qquad (-2)^4$$
$$-2^4 = -1 \times 2^4 = -16 \qquad\qquad (-2)^4 = (-1)^4 \times (2)^4 = 1 \times 16 = 16$$

As with a base of -1, any negative bases raised to an odd exponent will be negative, and any negative bases raised to an even exponent will be positive.

Combining Exponential Terms with Common Bases

The rules in this section *only* apply when the terms have the *same* base.

As you will see, all of these rules are related to the fact that exponents are shorthand for repeated multiplication.

Multiply Terms: Add Exponents

When *multiplying* two exponential terms with the same base, *add the exponents*. This rule is true no matter what the base is.

$$z^2 \times z^3 = (z \times z) \times (z \times z \times z) = z \times z \times z \times z \times z = z^5$$
$$4 \times 4^2 = (4) \times (4 \times 4) = 4 \times 4 \times 4 = 4^3$$

Fortunately, once you know the rule, you can simplify the computation greatly:

$$\left(\frac{1}{2}\right)^2 \times \left(\frac{1}{2}\right)^4 = \left(\frac{1}{2}\right)^{2+4} = \left(\frac{1}{2}\right)^6$$

Divide Terms: Subtract Exponents

When *dividing* two exponential terms with the same base, *subtract the exponents*. This rule is true no matter what the base is.

$$\frac{5^6}{5^2} = \frac{5 \times 5 \times 5 \times 5 \times \cancel{5} \times \cancel{5}}{\cancel{5} \times \cancel{5}} = 5 \times 5 \times 5 \times 5 = 5^4$$

Fortunately, once you know the rule, you can simplify the computation greatly:

$$\frac{x^{15}}{x^8} = x^{15-8} = x^7$$

Anything Raised to the Zero Equals 1

This rule is an extension of the previous rule. If you divide something by itself, the quotient is 1:

$$\frac{a^3}{a^3} = \frac{\not{a} \times \not{a} \times \not{a}}{\not{a} \times \not{a} \times \not{a}} = 1$$

Look at this division by subtracting exponents:

$$\frac{a^3}{a^3} = a^{3-3} = a^0$$

Therefore, $a^0 = 1$.

Any base raised to the 0 power equals 1. The one exception is a base of 0.

Note that 0^0 is *undefined.* That's because $\dfrac{0}{0}$ is undefined (but the GMAT does not test undefined numbers, so you don't need to memorize this).

Negative Exponents

The behavior of negative exponents is also an extension of the rules for dividing exponential terms.

$$\frac{y^2}{y^5} = \frac{y \times y}{y \times y \times y \times y \times y} = \frac{1}{y^3}$$

Look at this division by subtracting exponents:

$$\frac{y^2}{y^5} = y^{2-5} = y^{-3}$$

Therefore, $y^{-3} = \dfrac{1}{y^3}$.

This is the general rule: *something with a negative exponent is just "one over" that same thing with a positive exponent.* You can rewrite the above expression by taking the reciprocal of y^3 and dropping the negative sign.

Here are some additional examples of how to take the reciprocal and drop the negative sign:

$$\frac{1}{3^{-3}} = 3^3 \qquad\qquad \left(\frac{x}{4}\right)^{-2} = \frac{4^2}{x^2}$$

Nested Exponents: Multiply Exponents

How can you simplify $(z^2)^3$? Expand this term to show the repeated multiplication.

$$(z^2)^3 = (z^2) \times (z^2) \times (z^2) = z^{2+2+2} = z^6$$

When you raise an exponential term to an exponent, multiply the exponents.

$$(a^5)^4 = a^{5 \times 4} = a^{20}$$

Fractions and Exponents

There are four broad categories of fractions that all behave differently when raised to a power. The result depends on the size and the sign of the fraction, as well as on the power. While it is not necessary to memorize all of the cases below, it is important that you be able to re-create them when necessary.

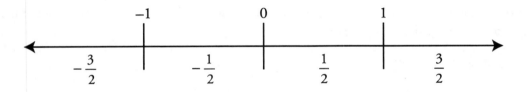

EVEN EXPONENTS (such as 2):

Less than −1	Between −1 and 0	Between 0 and 1	Greater than 1
$\left(-\dfrac{3}{2}\right)^2 = \dfrac{9}{4}$	$\left(-\dfrac{1}{2}\right)^2 = \dfrac{1}{4}$	$\left(\dfrac{1}{2}\right)^2 = \dfrac{1}{4}$	$\left(\dfrac{3}{2}\right)^2 = \dfrac{9}{4}$
$-\dfrac{3}{2} < \dfrac{9}{4}$	$-\dfrac{1}{2} < \dfrac{1}{4}$	$\dfrac{1}{2} > \dfrac{1}{4}$	$\dfrac{3}{2} < \dfrac{9}{4}$
Result is bigger.	Result is bigger.	Result is *smaller*.	Result is bigger.

ODD EXPONENTS (such as 3):

Less than −1	Between −1 and 0	Between 0 and 1	Greater than 1
$\left(-\dfrac{3}{2}\right)^3 = -\dfrac{27}{8}$	$\left(-\dfrac{1}{2}\right)^3 = -\dfrac{1}{8}$	$\left(\dfrac{1}{2}\right)^3 = \dfrac{1}{8}$	$\left(\dfrac{3}{2}\right)^3 = \dfrac{27}{8}$
$-\dfrac{3}{2} > -\dfrac{27}{8}$	$-\dfrac{1}{2} < -\dfrac{1}{8}$	$\dfrac{1}{2} > \dfrac{1}{8}$	$\dfrac{3}{2} < \dfrac{27}{8}$
Result is *smaller*.	Result is bigger.	Result is *smaller*.	Result is bigger.

As you can see, the effect of raising a fraction to a power varies depending upon the fraction's value, the sign, and the exponent.

To raise a fraction to a negative power, raise the reciprocal to the equivalent positive power.

$$\left(\frac{3}{7}\right)^{-2} = \left(\frac{7}{3}\right)^{2} = \frac{7^2}{3^2} = \frac{49}{9} \qquad \left(\frac{x}{y}\right)^{-w} = \left(\frac{y}{x}\right)^{w} = \frac{y^w}{x^w}$$

Factoring Out a Common Term

Normally, exponential terms that are added or subtracted cannot be combined. However, if two terms with the same base are added or subtracted, you can factor out a common term. For example:

$$11^3 + 11^4 \rightarrow 11^3(11^0 + 11^1) \rightarrow 11^3(1 + 11) \rightarrow 11^3(12)$$

On the GMAT, it generally pays to factor exponential terms that have bases in common.

If $x = 4^{20} + 4^{21} + 4^{22}$, what is the largest prime factor of x?

If you want to know the prime factors of x, you need to express x as a product. Factor 4^{20} out of the expression on the right side of the equation.

$$x = 4^{20} + 4^{21} + 4^{22}$$
$$x = 4^{20}(4^0 + 4^1 + 4^2)$$
$$x = 4^{20}(1 + 4 + 16)$$
$$x = 4^{20}(21)$$
$$x = 4^{20}(3 \times 7)$$

Now that you have expressed x as a product, you can see that 7 is the largest prime factor of x.

Equations with Exponents

Exponents can also appear in equations. In fact, the GMAT often complicates equations by including exponents or roots with unknown variables.

Here are a few situations to look out for when equations contain exponents.

Even Exponents Hide the Sign of the Base

Any number raised to an even exponent becomes positive. For example:

$$3^2 = 9 \qquad \text{AND} \qquad (-3)^2 = 9$$

Another way of saying this is that an even exponent hides the sign of its base. Compare the following two equations:

$$x^2 = 25 \qquad\qquad |x| = 5$$

MANHATTAN
PREP

Problem Set

Now that you've finished the chapter, do the following problems.

For problems 1 and 2, determine whether the inequality is TRUE or FALSE:

1. $\left(-\dfrac{3}{4}\right)^3 > -\dfrac{3}{4}$

2. $\left(\dfrac{x+1}{x}\right)^{-2} > \dfrac{x+1}{x}$, if $x > 0$.

3. $x^3 < x^2$. Describe the possible values of x.

4. Simplify: $\dfrac{m^8 p^7 r^{12}}{m^3 r^9 p} \times p^2 r^3 m^4$

5. If $p = \dfrac{x^{a+b}}{x^b}$, what is the value of positive integer p?

   (1) $x = 5$
   (2) $a = 0$

Save the below problem set for review, either after you finish this book or after you finish all of the Quant books that you plan to study.

6. Which of the following expressions has the largest value?

   (A) $(3^4)^{13}$ (B) $\left[(3^{30})^{12}\right]^{\frac{1}{10}}$ (C) $3^{30} + 3^{30} + 3^{30}$ (D) $4(3^{51})$ (E) $(3^{100})^{\frac{1}{2}}$

7. Simplify: $(4^y + 4^y + 4^y + 4^y)(3^y + 3^y + 3^y)$

   (A) $4^{4y} \times 3^{3y}$ (B) 12^{y+1} (C) $16^y \times 9^y$ (D) 12^y (E) $4^y \times 12^y$

8. If $4^a + 4^{a+1} = 4^{a+2} - 176$, what is the value of a?

9. If m and n are positive integers and $(2^{18})(5^m) = (20^n)$, what is the value of m?

10.　Which of the following is equivalent to $\left(\dfrac{1}{3}\right)^{-4}\left(\dfrac{1}{9}\right)^{-3}\left(\dfrac{1}{27}\right)^{-2}$?

(A) $\left(\dfrac{1}{3}\right)^{-8}$　　(B) $\left(\dfrac{1}{3}\right)^{-9}$　　(C) $\left(\dfrac{1}{3}\right)^{-16}$　　(D) $\left(\dfrac{1}{3}\right)^{-18}$　　(E) $\left(\dfrac{1}{3}\right)^{-144}$

11.　If $B^3A < 0$ and $A > 0$, which of the following must be negative?

(A) AB　　(B) B^2A　　(C) B^4　　(D) $\dfrac{A}{B^2}$　　(E) $-\dfrac{B}{A}$

4

Solutions

1. TRUE: Raising a proper fraction to a power causes that fraction to move closer to 0 on a number line. Raising any negative number to an odd power will result in a negative number. The number $\left(-\dfrac{3}{4}\right)^3$, therefore, will be to the right of $-\dfrac{3}{4}$ on the number line.

2. FALSE: Any number $\dfrac{x+1}{x}$, where x is positive, will be greater than 1. Therefore, raising that number to a negative exponent will result in a number smaller than 1 whenever x is a positive number:

$$\left(\frac{x+1}{x}\right)^{-2} = \left(\frac{x}{x+1}\right)^2 < \frac{x+1}{x}$$

3. Any non-zero number less than 1: As positive proper fractions are multiplied, their value decreases. For example, $\left(\dfrac{1}{2}\right)^3 < \left(\dfrac{1}{2}\right)^2$. Also, any negative number will make this inequality true. A negative number cubed is negative. Any negative number squared is positive. For example, $(-3)^3 < (-3)^2$. The number 0 itself, however, does not work, since $0^3 = 0^2$.

4. $m^9 p^8 r^6$: $\dfrac{m^8 p^7 r^{12}}{m^3 r^9 p} \times p^2 r^3 m^4 = \dfrac{m^{12} p^9 r^{15}}{m^3 r^9 p} = m^{(12-3)} p^{(9-1)} r^{(15-9)} = m^9 p^8 r^6$

5. (B): This question isn't really about p. It's about the expression $\dfrac{x^{a+b}}{x^b}$, which can be simplified by subtracting the exponent in the denominator from the exponent in the numerator:

$$\frac{x^{a+b}}{x^b} = x^{a+b-(b)} = x^a$$

So this question may be rephrased as simply, What is x^a?

Be careful, though—sufficiency in this case does *not* necessarily mean that you need to know x and a individually. (As just one example, if x is 1, then a is not needed, because 1 to any power is still 1.)

(1) INSUFFICIENT: Knowing that x is 5 is not sufficient without knowing a.

(2) SUFFICIENT: Anything to the 0 power is 1. The only exception to the rule is 0, because 0^0 is undefined. However, you have been told that p is a positive integer, so you know that x cannot equal 0.

The correct answer is **(B)**.

6. **(D):** Use the rules of exponents to simplify each expression:

(A) $(3^4)^{13} = 3^{52}$

(B) $\left[(3^{30})^{12}\right]^{\frac{1}{10}} = (3^{360})^{\frac{1}{10}} = 3^{\frac{360}{10}} = 3^{36}$

(C) $3^{30} + 3^{30} + 3^{30} = 3(3^{30}) = 3^{31}$

(D) $4(3^{51})$ cannot be simplified further.

(E) $(3^{100})^{\frac{1}{2}} = 3^{\frac{100}{2}} = 3^{50}$

Answer choice (A) is clearly larger than (B), (C), and (E). You must now compare $4(3^{51})$ to 3^{52}. To make them most easily comparable, factor one 3 out of 3^{52}: $3^{52} = 3(3^{51})$. Thus, $4(3^{51})$ is greater than $3(3^{51})$, so (D) is the correct answer.

7. **(B):** $(4^y + 4^y + 4^y + 4^y)(3^y + 3^y + 3^y) = (4 \times 4^y)(3 \times 3^y) = (4^{y+1})(3^{y+1}) = (4 \times 3)^{y+1} = (12)^{y+1}$

8. **2:** The key to this problem is to express all of the exponential terms in terms of the greatest common factor of the terms: 4^a. Using the addition rule (or the corresponding numerical examples), you get:

$$4^a + 4^{a+1} = 4^{a+2} - 176$$
$$176 = 4^{a+2} - 4^a - 4^{a+1}$$
$$176 = 4^a \times (4^2) - 4^a - 4^a \cdot (4^1)$$
$$176 = 4^a \times (4^2 - 4^0 - 4^1)$$
$$176 = 4^a \times (16 - 1 - 4)$$
$$176 = 4^a \times (11)$$
$$4^a = 176 \div 11 = 16$$
$$a = 2$$

9. **9:** With exponential equations such as this one, the key is to recognize that as long as the exponents are all integers, each side of the equation must have the same number of each type of prime factor. Break down each base into prime factors and set the exponents equal to each other:

$(2^{18})(5^m) = (20^n)$

$2^{18} \cdot 5^m = (2 \cdot 2 \cdot 5)^n$

$2^{18} \times 5^m = 2^{2n} \times 5^n$ $\longleftarrow$

$18 = 2n; \ m = n$

$n = 9; \ m = n = 9$

Because m and n have to be integers, there must be the **same number of 2's** on either side of the equation and there must be the **same number of 5's** on either side of the equation. Thus, $18 = 2n$ and $m = n$.

10. **(C):** Once again, you should break each base down into its prime factors first. Then, apply the negative exponent by taking the reciprocal of each term, and making the exponent positive:

$$\left(\frac{1}{3}\right)^{-4}\left(\frac{1}{9}\right)^{-3}\left(\frac{1}{27}\right)^{-2} = \left(\frac{1}{3}\right)^{-4}\left(\frac{1}{3^2}\right)^{-3}\left(\frac{1}{3^3}\right)^{-2} = 3^4 \times (3^2)^3 \times (3^3)^2 = 3^4 \times 3^6 \times 3^6 = 3^{4+6+6} = 3^{16}$$

Because all of the answer choices have negative exponents, you can perform the same transformation on them—simply take the reciprocal of each and change the exponent to a positive:

(A) $\left(\dfrac{1}{3}\right)^{-8} = 3^8$

(B) $\left(\dfrac{1}{3}\right)^{-9} = 3^9$

(C) $\left(\dfrac{1}{3}\right)^{-16} = 3^{16}$

(D) $\left(\dfrac{1}{3}\right)^{-18} = 3^{18}$

(E) $\left(\dfrac{1}{3}\right)^{-144} = 3^{144}$

4

11. **(A):** If A is positive, B^3 must be negative. Therefore, B must be negative. If A is positive and B is negative, the product AB must be negative.

Chapter *of* 5
Algebra

Roots

In This Chapter...

Memorize: Squares and Square Roots

Memorize the following squares and square roots, as they often appear on the GMAT.

$1^2 = 1$	$\sqrt{1} = 1$
$1.4^2 \approx 2$	$\sqrt{2} \approx 1.4$
$1.7^2 \approx 3$	$\sqrt{3} \approx 1.7$
$2.25^2 \approx 5$	$\sqrt{5} \approx 2.25$
$2^2 = 4$	$\sqrt{4} = 2$
$3^2 = 9$	$\sqrt{9} = 3$
$4^2 = 16$	$\sqrt{16} = 4$
$5^2 = 25$	$\sqrt{25} = 5$
$6^2 = 36$	$\sqrt{36} = 6$
$7^2 = 49$	$\sqrt{49} = 7$
$8^2 = 64$	$\sqrt{64} = 8$
$9^2 = 81$	$\sqrt{81} = 9$
$10^2 = 100$	$\sqrt{100} = 10$
$11^2 = 121$	$\sqrt{121} = 11$
$12^2 = 144$	$\sqrt{144} = 12$
$13^2 = 169$	$\sqrt{169} = 13$
$14^2 = 196$	$\sqrt{196} = 14$
$15^2 = 225$	$\sqrt{225} = 15$
$16^2 = 256$	$\sqrt{256} = 16$
$20^2 = 400$	$\sqrt{400} = 20$
$25^2 = 625$	$\sqrt{625} = 25$
$30^2 = 900$	$\sqrt{900} = 30$

5

Memorize: Cubes and Cube Roots

Memorize the following cubes and cube roots, as they often appear on the GMAT.

$1^3 = 1$	$\sqrt[3]{1} = 1$
$2^3 = 8$	$\sqrt[3]{8} = 2$
$3^3 = 27$	$\sqrt[3]{27} = 3$
$4^3 = 64$	$\sqrt[3]{64} = 4$
$5^3 = 125$	$\sqrt[3]{125} = 5$
$10^3 = 1,000$	$\sqrt[3]{1,000} = 10$

5

Problem Set

Now that you've finished the chapter, do the following problems.

1. For each of these statements, indicate whether the statement is TRUE or FALSE:

    (a) If $x^2 = 11$, then $x = \sqrt{11}$.
    (b) If $x^3 = 11$, then $x = \sqrt[3]{11}$.
    (c) If $x^4 = 16$, then $x = 2$.
    (d) If $x^5 = 32$, then $x = 2$.

Solve or simplify the following problems, using the properties of roots:

2. $\sqrt{18} \div \sqrt{2}$

3. Evaluate the following expression: $\left(\dfrac{4}{9}\right)^{-\frac{3}{2}}$

4. $\left(\dfrac{1}{81}\right)^{-\frac{1}{4}}$

5. $\sqrt{63} + \sqrt{28}$

6. $\sqrt[3]{100 - 36}$

Save the below problem set for review, either after you finish this book or after you finish all of the Quant books that you plan to study.

7. $\sqrt{150} - \sqrt{96}$

8. Estimate: $\sqrt{60}$

9. $\sqrt{20a} \times \sqrt{5a}$, assuming a is positive

10. $10\sqrt{12} \div 2\sqrt{3}$

11. $\sqrt{x^2 y^3 + 3x^2 y^3}$, assuming x and y are positive

12. $\sqrt{0.0081}$

13. $\dfrac{\sqrt[4]{64}}{\sqrt[4]{4}}$

Solutions

1. (a) **FALSE:** Even exponents hide the sign of the original number, because they always result in a positive value. If $x^2 = 11$, then $|x| = \sqrt{11}$. Thus, x could be either $\sqrt{11}$ or $-\sqrt{11}$.

(b) **TRUE:** Odd exponents preserve the sign of the original expression. Therefore, if x^3 is positive, then x must itself be positive. If $x^3 = 11$, then x must be $\sqrt[3]{11}$.

(c) **FALSE:** Even exponents hide the sign of the original number, because they always result in a positive value. If $x^4 = 16$, then x could be either 2 or -2.

(d) **TRUE:** Odd exponents preserve the sign of the original expression. Therefore, if x^5 is positive, then x must itself be positive. If $x^5 = 32$, then x must be 2.

2. **3:** $\sqrt{18} \div \sqrt{2} = \sqrt{9} = 3$

3. $\dfrac{27}{8}$: $\left(\dfrac{4}{9}\right)^{-\frac{3}{2}} = \left(\dfrac{9}{4}\right)^{\frac{3}{2}} = \sqrt{\left(\dfrac{9}{4}\right)^3} = \left(\sqrt{\dfrac{9}{4}}\right)^3 = \left(\dfrac{3}{2}\right)^3 = \dfrac{3^3}{2^3} = \dfrac{27}{8}$

4. **3:** $\left(\dfrac{1}{81}\right)^{-\frac{1}{4}} = 81^{\frac{1}{4}} = \sqrt[4]{81} = 3$

Note: On the GMAT, when given a square root symbol with a number beneath, you are supposed to take only the positive root. This restriction does not apply when given exponents (e.g., $x^2 = 16$ does give you both 4 and -4 as possible solutions).

5. $5\sqrt{7}$: $\sqrt{63} + \sqrt{28} = \left(\sqrt{9} \times \sqrt{7}\right) + \left(\sqrt{4} \times \sqrt{7}\right) = 3\sqrt{7} + 2\sqrt{7} = 5\sqrt{7}$

6. **4:** $\sqrt[3]{100 - 36} = \sqrt[3]{64} = 4$

7. $\sqrt{6}$: $\sqrt{150} - \sqrt{96} = \left(\sqrt{25} \times \sqrt{6}\right) - \left(\sqrt{16} \times \sqrt{6}\right) = 5\sqrt{6} - 4\sqrt{6} = \sqrt{6}$.

8. **7.7:** 60 is in between two perfect squares: 49, which is 7^2, and 64, which is 8^2. The difference between 64 and 49 is 15, so 60 is a little more than $\dfrac{2}{3}$ of the way toward 64 from 49. A reasonable estimate for $\sqrt{60}$, then, would be about 7.7, which is a little more than $\dfrac{2}{3}$ towards 8 from 7.

9. **10a:** $\sqrt{20a} \times \sqrt{5a} = \sqrt{100a^2} = 10a$

10. **10:** $10\sqrt{12} \div 2\sqrt{3} = \dfrac{10\left(\sqrt{4} \times \sqrt{3}\right)}{2\sqrt{3}} = \dfrac{20\sqrt{3}}{2\sqrt{3}} = 10$

11. $2xy\sqrt{y}$: Notice that you have two terms under the radical that both contain x^2y^3. You can add like terms together if they are under the same radical: $\sqrt{x^2y^3 + 3x^2y^3} = \sqrt{(1+3)x^2y^3} = \sqrt{4x^2y^3}$. Now, factor out all squares and isolate them under their own radical sign:

$$\sqrt{4x^2y^3} = \sqrt{4} \times \sqrt{x^2} \times \sqrt{y^2} \times \sqrt{y} = 2xy\sqrt{y}$$

(Note that since x and y are positive, $\sqrt{x^2} = x$ and $\sqrt{y^2} = y$.)

12. **0.09:** Since $(0.09)(0.09) = 0.0081$, $\sqrt{0.0081} = 0.09$. You can also rewrite 0.0081 as 81×10^{-4}:

$$\sqrt{81 \times 10^{-4}} = \sqrt{81} \times \sqrt{10^{-4}} = 9 \times (10^{-4})^{\frac{1}{2}} = 9 \times 10^{-2} = 0.09$$

13. **2:** $\dfrac{\sqrt[4]{64}}{\sqrt[4]{4}} = \sqrt[4]{\dfrac{64}{4}} = \sqrt[4]{16} = 2$

Chapter 6
of Algebra

Quadratic Equations

In This Chapter...

Chapter 6

Quadratic Equations

One special type of exponent equation is called the quadratic equation. Here are some examples of quadratic equations:

$$x^2 + 3x + 8 = 12 \qquad w^2 - 16w + 1 = 0 \qquad 2y^2 - y + 5 = 8$$

The standard form of a quadratic equation is $ax^2 + bx + c = 0$, where a, b, and c are constants and a does not equal 0.

Here are other ways of writing quadratics (in non-standard form):

$$x^2 = 3x + 4 \qquad a = 5a^2 \qquad 6 - b = 7b^2$$

Like other even exponent equations, quadratic equations generally have two solutions. That is, there are usually two possible values of x (or whatever the variable is) that make the equation *true*.

Factoring Quadratic Equations

The following example illustrates the process for solving quadratic equations:

Given that $x^2 + 3x + 8 = 12$, what is x?

To start, move all the terms to the left side of the equation, combine them, and put them in the form $ax^2 + bx + c$ (where a, b, and c are integers). The right side of the equation should be set to 0:

$$x^2 + 3x + 8 = 12 \qquad$$ Subtracting 12 from both sides of the equation puts all the
$$x^2 + 3x - 4 = 0 \qquad$$ terms on the left side and sets the right side to 0.

Next, factor the equation. In order to factor, you generally need to think about two terms in the equation. Assuming that $a = 1$ (which is usually the case on GMAT quadratic equation problems), focus on the two terms b and c. (If a is not equal to 1, simply divide the equation through by a.)

> In the equation $x^2 + 3x - 4 = 0$, $b = 3$ and $c = -4$. In order to factor this equation, you need to find two integers whose product is -4 and whose sum is 3. The only two integers that work are 4 and -1, since $4(-1) = -4$ and $4 + (-1) = 3$.

Now, rewrite the equation in the form $(x + ?)(x + ?)$, where the question marks represent the two integers you solved for in the previous step:

$$x^2 + 3x - 4 = 0$$
$$(x + 4)(x - 1) = 0$$

> The left side of the equation is now a product of two factors in parentheses: $(x + 4)$ and $(x - 1)$. Since this product equals 0, one or both of the factors must be 0.

> For instance, if you know that $M \times N = 0$, then you know that either $M = 0$ or $N = 0$ (or both M and N are 0).

> In this problem, set each factor in parentheses independently to 0 and solve for x:

$$x + 4 = 0 \qquad \text{OR} \qquad x - 1 = 0$$
$$x = -4 \qquad\qquad\qquad x = 1$$

Therefore, the two solutions or roots of the quadratic equation $x^2 + 3x + 8 = 12$ are -4 and 1.

Disguised Quadratics

The GMAT will often attempt to disguise quadratic equations by putting them in forms that do not quite look like the traditional form of $ax^2 + bx + c = 0$.

Here is a very common "disguised" form for a quadratic:

$$3w^2 = 6w$$

This is certainly a quadratic equation. However, it is very tempting to try to solve this equation without thinking of it as a quadratic. This classic mistake looks like this:

$3w^2 = 6w$ Divide both sides by w.
$3w = 6$ Divide both sides by 3.
$w = 2$

If you solve this equation without factoring it like a quadratic, you will miss one of the solutions! Here is how it should be solved:

$$3w^2 = 6w$$
$$3w^2 - 6w = 0$$
$$w(3w - 6) = 0$$

Setting both factors equal to 0 yields the following solutions:

$$3w - 6 = 0$$
$$w = 0 \qquad \text{OR} \qquad 3w = 6$$
$$w = 2$$

If you recognize that $3w^2 = 6w$ is a disguised quadratic, you will find both solutions instead of accidentally missing one (in this case, the solution $w = 0$).

Here is another example of a disguised quadratic:

Solve for b, given that $\dfrac{36}{b} = b - 5$.

At first glance, this does not look like a quadratic equation. The first simplification step is to get rid of that fraction. Watch what happens:

$$\frac{36}{b} = b - 5 \qquad \text{Multiply both sides of the equation by } b.$$

$$36 = b^2 - 5b$$

Now this looks like a quadratic! Solve it by factoring:

$$36 = b^2 - 5b \quad \text{Subtract 36 from both sides to set the equation equal to 0.}$$
$$b^2 - 5b - 36 = 0$$
$$(b - 9)(b + 4) = 0 \qquad \text{Thus, } b = 9 \text{ or } b = -4.$$

Some quadratics are hidden within more difficult equations, such as higher order equations (in which a variable is raised to the power of 3 or more). On the GMAT, these equations can almost always be factored to find the hidden quadratic expression. For example:

Solve for x, given that $x^3 + 2x^2 - 3x = 0$.

$$x^3 + 2x^2 - 3x = 0 \qquad \text{Factor out an } x \text{ from each term.}$$
$$x(x^2 + 2x - 3) = 0$$

Now factor the quadratic:

$$x(x^2 + 2x - 3) = 0$$
$$x(x + 3)(x - 1) = 0 \qquad x = 0 \quad \text{OR} \quad x + 3 = 0 \quad \text{OR} \quad x - 1 = 0.$$

This equation has *three* solutions: 0, −3, and 1.

This example illustrates a general rule:

> If you have a quadratic expression equal to 0, *and* you can factor an x out of the expression, then $x = 0$ is a solution of the equation.

Do not just divide both sides by x. If you do so, you will eliminate the solution $x = 0$. You are only allowed to divide by a variable if you are absolutely sure that the variable does not equal 0.

Taking the Square Root

So far you have seen how to solve quadratic equations by setting one side of the equation equal to 0 and factoring. However, some quadratic problems can be solved without setting one side equal to 0. If the other side of the equation is a perfect square, the problem can be solved by taking the square root of both sides of the equation. For example:

If $(z + 3)^2 = 25$, what is z?

You could solve this problem by distributing the left-hand side of the equation, setting the right-hand side equal to 0, and factoring. However, it would be much easier to take the square root of both sides of the equation to solve for z. You just have to consider both the positive and the negative square root:

$$\sqrt{(z+3)^2} = \sqrt{25}$$
$$z + 3 = \pm 5$$
$$z = -3 \pm 5$$
$$z = \{2, -8\}$$

Going in Reverse: Use FOIL

Instead of starting with a quadratic equation and factoring it, you may need to start with factors and rewrite them as a quadratic equation. To do this, use a multiplication process called FOIL: First, Outer, Inner, Last.

To change the expression $(x + 7)(x - 3)$ into a quadratic equation, use FOIL as follows:

First: Multiply the <u>first term</u> of each factor together: $x \times x = x^2$

Outer: Multiply the <u>outer terms</u> of the expression together: $x(-3) = -3x$

Inner: Multiply the <u>inner terms</u> of the expression together: $7(x) = 7x$

Last: Multiply the <u>last term</u> of each factor together: $7(-3) = -21$

Now, there are four terms: $x^2 - 3x + 7x - 21$. By combining the two middle terms, you have your quadratic expression: $x^2 + 4x - 21$.

If you encounter a quadratic equation or expression, try factoring it. On the other hand, if you encounter the product of factors such as $(x + 7)(x - 3)$, you may need to use FOIL. Note that if the product of factors equals 0, you should be ready to *interpret* the meaning. For instance, if you are given $(x + k)(x - m) = 0$, then you know that $x = -k$ or $x = m$.

One-Solution Quadratics

Not all quadratic equations have two solutions. Some have only one solution. One-solution quadratics are also called perfect square quadratics, because both roots are the same. Consider the following examples:

$$x^2 + 8x + 16 = 0$$
$$(x + 4)(x + 4) = 0$$
$$(x + 4)^2 = 0 \qquad \text{Here, the only solution for } x \text{ is } -4.$$

$$x^2 - 6x + 9 = 0$$
$$(x - 3)(x - 3) = 0$$
$$(x - 3)^2 = 0 \qquad \text{Here, the only solution for } x \text{ is } 3.$$

When you see a quadratic equation, look for two solutions, but be aware that some circumstances will lead to just one solution. As long as you understand how the math works, you'll know when you should have two solutions and when you should have just one.

Zero in the Denominator: Undefined

When 0 appears in the denominator of an expression, then that expression is called *undefined*. How does this convention affect quadratic equations? Consider the following:

What are the solutions to the following equation?

$$\frac{x^2 + x - 12}{x - 2} = 0$$

The numerator contains a quadratic equation. Since it is a good idea to start solving quadratic equations by factoring, factor this numerator as follows:

$$\frac{x^2 + x - 12}{x - 2} = 0 \quad \rightarrow \quad \frac{(x-3)(x+4)}{x-2} = 0$$

If either of the factors in the numerator is 0, then the entire expression equals 0. Thus, the solutions to this equation are $x = 3$ or $x = -4$.

Note that making the denominator of the fraction equal to 0 would *not* make the entire expression equal to 0. Recall that if 0 appears in the denominator, the expression becomes undefined. Thus, $x = 2$ (which would make the denominator equal to 0) is *not* a solution to this equation. In fact, since setting x equal to 2 would make the denominator 0, the value 2 is illegal: x *cannot* equal 2.

The Three Special Products

Three quadratic expressions called *special products* come up so frequently on the GMAT that it pays to memorize them. They are GMAT favorites! Make yourself some flash cards and drill them until you immediately recognize these three expressions and know how to factor (or distribute) each one automatically. This will usually put you on the path toward the solution to the problem.

Special Product #1:	$x^2 - y^2 = (x + y)(x - y)$	**Memorize these!**
Special Product #2:	$x^2 + 2xy + y^2 = (x + y)(x + y) = (x + y)^2$	
Special Product #3:	$x^2 - 2xy + y^2 = (x - y)(x - y) = (x - y)^2$	

You may also need to identify these products when they are presented in other forms. For example, $a^2 - 1$ can be factored as $(a + 1)(a - 1)$. Similarly, $(a + b)^2$ can be distributed as $a^2 + 2ab + b^2$.

Within an equation, you may need to recognize these special products in pieces. For instance, if you see $a^2 + b^2 = 9 + 2ab$, move the $2ab$ term to the left, yielding $a^2 - 2ab + b^2 = 9$. This quadratic can then be factored to $(a - b)^2 = 9$, or $a - b = \pm 3$.

Simplify: $\dfrac{x^2 + 4x + 4}{x^2 - 4}$, given that x does not equal 2 or –2.

Both the numerator and denominator of this fraction can be factored:

$$\frac{(x + 2)(x + 2)}{(x + 2)(x - 2)}$$

The expression $x + 2$ can be cancelled out from the numerator and denominator:

$$\frac{x^2 + 4x + 4}{x^2 - 4} = \frac{x + 2}{x - 2}$$

MANHATTAN
PREP

Problem Set

Now that you've finished the chapter, do the following problems.

1. $(3-\sqrt{7})(3+\sqrt{7})=$

2. If -4 is a solution for x in the equation $x^2 + kx + 8 = 0$, what is k?

3. If 8 and -4 are the solutions for x, which of the following could be the equation?

    (A) $x^2 - 4x - 32 = 0$ (B) $x^2 - 4x + 32 = 0$ (C) $x^2 + 4x - 12 = 0$
    (D) $x^2 + 4x + 32 = 0$ (E) $x^2 + 4x + 12 = 0$

4. If $x^2 + k = G$ and x is an integer, which of the following could be the value of $G - k$?

    (A) 7   (B) 8   (C) 9   (D) 10   (E) 11

5. What is x?

    (1) $x = 4y - 4$
    (2) $xy = 8$

Save the below problem set for review, either after you finish this book or after you finish all of the Quant books that you plan to study.

6. Given that $\dfrac{d}{4} + \dfrac{8}{d} + 3 = 0$, what is d?

7. Given that $\dfrac{x^2 + 6x + 9}{x + 3} = 7$, what is x?

8. Given that $(p - 3)^2 - 5 = 0$, what is p?

9. Given that $z^2 - 10z + 25 = 9$, what is z?

10. Hugo lies on top of a building, throwing pennies straight down to the street below. The formula for the height, H, that a penny falls is $H = Vt + 5t^2$, where V is the original velocity of the penny (how fast Hugo throws it when it leaves his hand) and t is equal to the time it takes to hit the ground. The building is 60 meters high, and Hugo throws the penny down at an initial speed of 20 meters per second. How long does it take for the penny to hit the ground?

11. If $a \neq 2$, which of the following is equal to $\dfrac{b(a^2 - 4)}{ab - 2b}$?

    (A) ab (B) a (C) $a + 2$ (D) a^2 (E) $2b$

6

Solutions

1. **2:** Use FOIL to simplify this product:

F: $3 \times 3 = 9$

O: $3 \times \sqrt{7} = 3\sqrt{7}$

I: $-\sqrt{7} \times 3 = -3\sqrt{7}$

L: $-\sqrt{7} \times \sqrt{7} = -7$

$9 + 3\sqrt{7} - 3\sqrt{7} - 7 = 2$

Alternatively, recognize that the original expression is in the form $(x - y)(x + y)$, which is one of the three special products and which equals $x^2 - y^2$ (the difference of two squares). Thus, the expression simplifies to $3^2 - (\sqrt{7})^2 = 9 - 7 = 2$.

2. **6:** If -4 is a solution, then you know that $(x + 4)$ must be one of the factors of the quadratic equation. The other factor is $(x + ?)$. You know that the product of 4 and ? must be equal to 8; thus, the other factor is $(x + 2)$. You know that the sum of 4 and 2 must be equal to k. Therefore, $k = 6$.

Alternatively, if -4 is a solution, then it is a possible value for x. Plug it into the equation for x and solve for k:

$$x^2 + kx + 8 = 0$$
$$16 - 4k + 8 = 0$$
$$24 = 4k$$
$$k = 6$$

3. **(A):** If the solutions to the equation are 8 and -4, the factored form of the equation is: $(x - 8)(x + 4) = 0$

Use FOIL to find the quadratic form: $x^2 - 4x - 32 = 0$. Therefore, the correct equation is (A).

4. **(C):** $x^2 + k = G$

$x^2 = G - k$

Because you know that x is an integer, x^2 is a perfect square (the square of an integer). Therefore, $G - k$ is also a perfect square. The only perfect square among the answer choices is (C), 9.

5. **(E):** Each statement alone is not enough information to solve for x. Using statements (1) and (2) combined, if you substitute the expression for x in the first equation, into the second, you get two different answers:

$$x = 4y - 4$$
$$xy = (4y - 4)y = 8$$
$$4y^2 - 4y = 8$$
$$y^2 - y - 2 = 0$$
$$(y + 1)(y - 2) = 0$$

$$y = \{-1, 2\}$$
$$x = \{-8, 4\}$$

6. **{−8, −4}:** Multiply the entire equation by $4d$ (to eliminate the denominators) and factor:

$$d^2 + 32 + 12d = 0$$
$$d^2 + 12d + 32 = 0$$
$$(d + 8)(d + 4) = 0$$

$$d + 8 = 0 \qquad \text{OR} \qquad d + 4 = 0$$
$$d = -8 \qquad\qquad\qquad d = -4$$

7. **4:** Cross-multiply, simplify, and factor to solve:

$$\frac{x^2 + 6x + 9}{x + 3} = 7$$
$$x^2 + 6x + 9 = 7x + 21$$
$$x^2 - x - 12 = 0$$
$$(x + 3)(x - 4) = 0$$

$$x + 3 = 0 \qquad \text{OR} \qquad x - 4 = 0$$
$$x = -3 \qquad\qquad\qquad x = 4$$

Discard −3 as a value for x, since this value would make the denominator 0; thus, the fraction would be undefined.

8. **{3 + √5, 3 − √5}:**

$$(p - 3)^2 - 5 = 0$$
$$(p - 3)^2 = 5$$
$$\sqrt{(p-3)^2} = \sqrt{5}$$
$$p - 3 = \pm\sqrt{5}$$
$$p = 3 \pm \sqrt{5}$$

Note that if you try to distribute out $(p - 3)^2$ and solve as a quadratic, you will realize there is a non-integer solution and you can't easily solve that way. You would get:

$$p^2 - 6p + 9 - 5 = 0$$
$$p^2 - 6p + 4 = 0$$

There aren't any integers that multiply to 4 and add to 6; at this point, you could choose to use the quadratic equation to solve or you could solve using the method shown at the beginning of this explanation.

9. **{2, 8}:** Since you recognize that the left-hand side of the equation is a perfect square quadratic, you will factor the left side of the equation first, instead of trying to set everything equal to 0.

$$z^2 - 10z + 25 = 9$$
$$(z-5)^2 = 9$$
$$\sqrt{(z-5)^2} = \sqrt{9}$$
$$z - 5 = \pm 3$$
$$z = 5 \pm 3$$

10. **2:**

$$H = Vt + 5t^2$$
$$60 = 20t + 5t^2$$
$$5t^2 + 20t - 60 = 0$$
$$5(t^2 + 4t - 12) = 0$$
$$5(t+6)(t-2) = 0$$

$t + 6 = 0$ OR $t - 2 = 0$ Since a time must be positive, discard the
$t = -6$ $t = 2$ negative value for t.

11. **(C):** Choose numbers. The number 2 is not allowed and the number 4 appears in the expression, so try plugging $a = 3$ and $b = 5$ into the expression:

$$\frac{b(a^2 - 4)}{ab - 2b} =$$

$$\frac{(5)((3)^2 - 4)}{(3)(5) - 2(5)} =$$

$$\frac{5(9 - 4)}{15 - 10} =$$

$$\frac{5(5)}{5} = 5$$

Now, plug $a = 3$ and $b = 5$ into the answer choices and look for a matching answer of 5:

(A) $ab = (3)(5) = 15$
(B) $a = (3) = 3$
(C) $a + 2 = (3) + 2 = 5$ Match!
(D) $a^2 = (3)^2 = 9$
(E) $2b = 2(5) = 10$

The correct answer is **(C)**.

Alternatively, solve algebraically. Begin by factoring the given expression, then simplify:

$$\frac{b(a+2)(a-2)}{b(a-2)} = a+2$$

Everything divides out except for the $a + 2$ term. If you spot that quickly, then the algebraic solution is faster. If not, then the smart numbers solution may be faster.

MANHATTAN
PREP

Chapter 7
of Algebra

Strategy: Combos

In This Chapter...

Chapter 7

Strategy: Combos

Combo problems look, at first glance, much like certain algebra questions you learned in school.

What is the value of $\dfrac{x}{y}$?

(1) $\dfrac{x+y}{y} = 3$

(2) $y = 4$

It wasn't unusual to be asked, in school, to solve for $\dfrac{x}{y}$, or $x + y$, or any similar combination of variables. Find x, find y, and voilà! You can calculate any combination of the variables, too.

GMAT combo problems however, have one key difference: your goal is to solve directly for the *combination* of variables, not for each individual variable.

How to Solve for Combos

Here's how to solve for combos in the above problem:

Step 1: Notice that the question asks for a combo.

When a question asks directly for a combination of variables, you have a combo problem. (There are ways to disguise a combo—you'll see an example later in this chapter.)

Step 2: Manipulate any given information to try to match the combo.

The question stem doesn't contain any given information. The question itself is already simplified: $\dfrac{x}{y} = ?$

Jump into the statements:

(1) $\dfrac{x+y}{y} = 3$

If you weren't looking for the combo, you might do something like this: $x + y = 3y$. The combo contains a fraction $\left(\dfrac{x}{y}\right)$, so you actually do not want to get rid of that denominator. How else can you manipulate the equation while preserving the fraction? Try splitting the numerator:

$$\dfrac{x}{y} + \dfrac{y}{y} = 3$$

Bingo! The fraction on the left matches the combo and the one on the right goes away:

$$\dfrac{x}{y} + 1 = 3$$

$$\dfrac{x}{y} = 2$$

Statement (1) is actually sufficient!   AD
                                           ~~BCE~~

7

Note that you cannot find the individual values for x and y from this statement. If you follow your "school" instincts and try to solve for each variable, you'll answer this question incorrectly. Always try to solve for the combo.

Here's statement (2):

(2) $y = 4$

The statement provides no information about x, so it is not sufficient. The correct answer is **(A)**.   Ⓐ~~D~~
                                                                                                                ~~BCE~~

When you solve for a combo in Data Sufficiency (DS), your ultimate goal is to try to find a single match for the desired combo. If you can, then the statement is sufficient.

The above problem also contains a common DS trap called the C-trap. Problems with this trap appear to work when both statements are used together—that is, the answer appears to be (C). In actuality, one of the two statements works by itself and (C) is incorrect. Take a look at the two statements again:

(1) $\dfrac{x+y}{y} = 3$

(2) $y = 4$

If you are trying to solve for x and y individually, you will realize pretty quickly that neither statement alone will get you there. Put the two statements together, however, and it is possible to find the values of both x and y.

There's just one hitch: the problem didn't ask for the values of x and y. It asked for the value of $\frac{x}{y}$, and statement (1) is sufficient all by itself to find that combo.

Keep an eye out for the C-trap on Data Sufficiency. If it is obvious that the two statements do work together, reexamine each one individually; one might work all by itself. Combo problems are a very common place for C-traps to occur.

Try another combo problem:

> If $x \neq y$, what is the value of $x + y$?
>
> (1) $x - y = 1$
>
> (2) $x^2 - y^2 = x - y$

Step 1: Notice that the question asks for a combo.

The question stem asks directly for a combo: $x + y$.

Step 2: Manipulate any given information to try to match the combo

Write down $x \neq y$ on your scrap paper. You may or may not have to use this piece of information, but either way, you don't want to forget it. Now look at statement (1):

> (1) $x - y = 1$

Hmm. How can you turn this into $x + y$? How about $x = y + 1$. Good, now there's an addition sign— but it's not between the x and y. What next?

It turns out that, no matter how you manipulate the equation, you can't change the original subtraction relationship between x and y. As a general rule, if you are given just one linear equation with only basic math operations (addition, subtraction, multiplication, or division), you cannot alter the initial relationship between the two variables. If it starts out as subtraction, it will remain subtraction, no matter what you do to the equation.

This statement is not sufficient; cross off answers (A) and (D).

$$\begin{array}{c} \text{A\!D} \\ \text{BCE} \end{array}$$

Now look at statement (2):

> (2) $x^2 - y^2 = x - y$

This one must also not work, since it also has $x - y$, right? Hang on. This one also contains some other terms. What can you do with them?

If you have already memorized the three special products, you'll recognize $x^2 - y^2$. If you haven't yet done so, make a flash card for yourself right now and start drilling.

As a general rule, whenever you see one of the special products, write down the given form *and* the other form:

$$x^2 - y^2 \Leftrightarrow (x+y)(x-y)$$

Substitute the other form into the given equation:

$$(x+y)(x-y) = x - y$$

What next?

The expression $(x-y)$ appears on both sides of the equation. You can divide it out as long as you know that it does not equal 0. That's why the question stem says that $x \neq y$! If so, then $x - y$ cannot equal 0. Divide both sides of the equation by $(x-y)$:

$$(x+y) = 1$$

This statement is sufficient to answer the question. The answer is **(B)**.   ~~AD~~
                                                                                ⒷCE

In sum:

Step 1: Notice that the question asks for a combo.

A question stem may ask for the combo directly or it may try to disguise the question (see the next section for more).

Step 2: Manipulate any given information to try to match the combo.

Your goal is to try to match the combination of variables. Most of the time, if you try to solve for each variable individually, you will get the question wrong. Go for the combo!

When to Solve for Combos

Whenever the problem asks you for a combination, try to solve directly for it. Sometimes, a question stem will obviously ask for a combo; other times, the question will come in disguise.

Try this problem:

> If $a = 3bc$ and $abc \neq 0$, what is the value of c?
>
> (1) $a = 10 - b$
> (2) $3a = 4b$

This question definitely does *not* look like a combo question. This time, though, the question stem also contains a given equation: $a = 3bc$. Solve this for c:

$$c = \frac{a}{3b}$$

What would you need to know in order to calculate c? Take a look at the equation this way:

$$c = \left(\frac{1}{3}\right)\left(\frac{a}{b}\right)$$

In other words, if you can find a value for the combination $\frac{a}{b}$, then you can calculate c. This problem is a combo problem in disguise!

Step 1: Notice that the question asks for a combo.

If the question stem contains given information in addition to a question that asks for a single variable, see how the information can be combined. It's possible that you have a combo question in disguise.

Step 2: Manipulate any given information to try to match the combo. Look at statement (1):

> (1) $a = 10 - b$

Is there any way to find a value for $\frac{a}{b}$? First, put the variables on the same side of the equals sign: $a + b = 10$. There's no way to turn an addition relationship into a division relationship without further information.

This statement is not sufficient to answer the question. Now look at statement (2):

~~AD~~
BCE

> (2) $3a = 4b$

Get the variables on the same side:

$$\frac{3a}{4b} = 1$$

Perfect: a division relationship! If you aren't sure, take one more step to solve, but if you can see that you will be able to find a value for $\frac{a}{b}$, then you're done:

$$\frac{a}{b} = \frac{4}{3}$$

This statement is sufficient; the correct answer is **(B)**.   ~~AD~~
ⒷCE

How to Get Better at Combos

To get better at combos, practice the problems at the end of this chapter. When the question doesn't obviously ask for a combination of variables, ask yourself what to do to strip off the disguise and find the combo.

Afterwards, review the problem. In particular, see whether you can articulate both how to reveal the combo (where necessary) and how to find a match or prove that no match exists. Could you explain to a fellow student who is confused?

If so, then you are starting to learn both the process by which you use combos and the underlying principles that these kinds of problems test. You're ready to try *Official Guide* problems or move on to other topics.

If not, then review the solution, search online, or ask an instructor or fellow student for help. When doing *OG* problems, review the solutions in our GMAT Navigator™ program.

7

Strategy: Combos   Chapter 7

Problem Set

1. What is the sum of x, y, and z?

    $x + y = 8$
    $x + z = 11$
    $y + z = 7$

2. If x and y are integers, what is $x + y$?

    (1) $3^x = 81$

    (2) $5^x = \dfrac{25}{5^y}$

3. If x and y are integers, what is the value of $x^2 + 2xy + y^2$?

    (1) $x + y = 7$

    (2) $2x = \dfrac{28 - 4y}{2}$

4. If $xy \neq 0$ and $\sqrt{\dfrac{xy}{3}} = x$, what is y?

    (1) $\dfrac{x}{y} = \dfrac{1}{3}$

    (2) $x = 3$

5. If $A = \dfrac{\dfrac{x}{3}}{\dfrac{2}{y}}$, what is A?

    (1) $xy = 8$

    (2) $\dfrac{x}{y} = 2$

6. If $x = \dfrac{9b - 3ab}{\dfrac{3}{a} - \dfrac{a}{3}}$, what is x?

    (1) $\dfrac{9ab}{3 + a} = \dfrac{18}{5}$

    (2) $b = 1$

103

Solutions

1. **13:** It is possible to solve for x, y, and z individually, but you will save a significant amount of time by solving for the combo. What is $x + y + z$?

The equations collectively contain exactly two "copies" of each variable and these variables are always added. Add the three equations together:

$$\begin{array}{rrrl} x + & y & & = 8 \\ x & & + z & = 11 \\ + & y + & z & = 7 \\ \hline 2x + & 2y + & 2z & = 26 \end{array}$$

Divide the equation by 2: $x + y + z = 13$.

2. **(B):** The question asks for the combo $x + y$ and specifies that x and y are integers.

(1) INSUFFICIENT: $3^x = 81$

You could solve for the value of x, but the statement does not provide any information about the value of y, so this statement is not sufficient. Don't solve for x now; check statement (2) first.

(2) SUFFICIENT:

$$5^x = \frac{25}{5^y}$$

$$(5^x)(5^y) = 25$$
$$5^{x+y} = 5^2$$
$$x + y = 2$$

Note that, if you do not do the math (or you do it incorrectly), you may think that this statement is not enough to answer the question. In that case, you may have fallen into a C-trap: the two statements together are definitely enough, but the answer cannot be (C) because one of the statements works by itself.

The correct answer is **(B)**.

3. **(D):** The question stem specifies that x and y are integers and asks for the value of $x^2 + 2xy + y^2$. Since the expression is one of the common quadratic identities, write down its other form as well: $(x + y)^2$.

(1) SUFFICIENT: The work is made much easier if you recognized the quadratic identity and wrote down both forms. Knowing the value of $x + y$ is enough to find the value of $(x + y)^2$.

(2) SUFFICIENT:

$$2x = \frac{28 - 4y}{2}$$

$$4x = 28 - 4y$$
$$4x + 4y = 28$$
$$x + y = 7$$

The correct answer is **(D)**.

4. **(B):** The question asks for the value of y, so isolate y in the given equation:

$$\sqrt{\frac{xy}{3}} = x$$

$$\frac{xy}{3} = x^2$$

$$xy = 3x^2 \quad \text{It's okay to divide by } x \text{ since you know that } x \text{ is not } 0.$$

$$y = 3x$$

In other words, if you can find the value of x, then you can also find the value of y.

(1) INSUFFICIENT: Statement (1) provides the value of $\frac{x}{y}$, but does not provide the value of x and y individually. For example, x could be 1 and y could be 3, or x could be 2 and y could be 6. Ironically, the combo is not helpful here since this same combo is given in the stem.

(2) SUFFICIENT: With x, you can find y using the rephrased equation from the question stem.

This problem is a reminder that sometimes what appears to be a combo question might just involve "school" algebra of solving for a single variable.

The correct answer is **(B)**.

5. **(A):** This question is a combo problem in disguise. The question asks for A, but the value of A is dependent upon x and y. Before diving into the statements, simplify the given equation:

$$A = \frac{\dfrac{x}{3}}{\dfrac{2}{y}}$$

$$A = \frac{x}{3} \times \frac{y}{2}$$

$$A = \frac{xy}{6}$$

If you can find the value of xy, you will have enough information to answer the question.

(1) SUFFICIENT: Statement (1) matches the rephrased question, so it is sufficient to answer the question.

(2) INSUFFICIENT: It is not possible to find the value for xy from the value for $\dfrac{x}{y}$. For example, x could be 2 and y could be 1, in which case xy is 2. Alternatively, x could be 4 and y could be 2, in which case xy is 8. Put differently, the quotient combo and the product combo are not one in the same.

The correct answer is **(A)**.

6. **(A):** This question is really a combo problem in disguise. Notice that the question asks for x, and the question stem contains an equation with x. You need to simplify the expression on the right side of the equation to solve for the simplest combo possible. As a general rule, simplify fractions as much as possible (eliminate them entirely if possible). Also as a general rule, if the same variable exists in more than one place in the question, attempt to combine like terms.

Begin by getting a common denominator on the bottom:

$$x = \frac{9b - 3ab}{\dfrac{3}{a} - \dfrac{a}{3}} = \frac{9b - 3ab}{\dfrac{9}{3a} - \dfrac{a^2}{3a}} = \frac{9b - 3ab}{\dfrac{9 - a^2}{3a}}$$

Now that you have only a single fraction on the bottom, you can flip it over (thus multiplying the numerator by the reciprocal of the denominator):

$$9b - 3ab \times \frac{3a}{9 - a^2} = \frac{3a(9b - 3ab)}{9 - a^2}$$

A lot of factoring can be done here! Factor the common term $3b$ out of the parentheses in the numerator, and factor the denominator as the difference of squares:

$$\frac{3a(9b - 3ab)}{9 - a^2} = \frac{3a(3b)(3 - a)}{(3 - a)(3 + a)}$$

Cancel $(3 - a)$ from both the top and the bottom:

$$\frac{3a(3b)}{(3 + a)} = \frac{9ab}{3 + a}$$

7

Thus, the question is, "What is the value of $\dfrac{9ab}{3+a}$?" You can solve the statements directly for this combo.

(1) SUFFICIENT: This statement directly gives you the value of the combo.

(2) INSUFFICIENT: Knowing the value of b does not give you the value of the combo $\dfrac{9ab}{3+a}$.

The correct answer is **(A)**.

Chapter 8

of

Algebra

Formulas

In This Chapter...

Chapter 8

Formulas

Formulas are another means by which the GMAT tests your ability to work with unknowns. Formulas are specific equations that can involve multiple variables. There are four major types of formula problems on the GMAT:

1. Plug-in formulas
2. Functions
3. Strange symbol formulas
4. Sequence formulas

The GMAT uses formulas both in abstract problems and in real-life word problems.

Plug-in Formulas

The most basic GMAT formula problems provide you with a formula and ask you to solve for one of the variables in the formula by plugging in given values for the other variables. For example:

> The formula for determining an individual's comedic aptitude, C, on a given day
> is defined as $\dfrac{QL}{J}$, where J represents the number of jokes told, Q represents the
> overall joke quality on a scale of 1 to 10, and L represents the number of individual
> laughs generated. If Nicole told 12 jokes, generated 18 laughs, and earned a co-
> medic aptitude of 10.5, what was the overall quality of her jokes?

Plug the given values into the formula in order to solve for the unknown variable Q:

$$C = \frac{QL}{J} \quad \rightarrow \quad 10.5 = \frac{18Q}{12} \quad \rightarrow \quad Q = \frac{10.5(12)}{18} \quad \rightarrow \quad Q = \frac{10.5(2)}{3} \quad \rightarrow \quad \frac{21}{3} \quad \rightarrow \quad Q = 7$$

The quality of Nicole's jokes was rated a 7.

Notice that you will typically have to do some rearrangement after plugging in the numbers in order to isolate the desired unknown. The actual computations are typically not very complex (though do remember to simplify before you multiply!). Formula problems are tricky because the given formula is unfamiliar. Do not be intimidated. Write the equation down, plug in the numbers carefully, and solve for the required unknown.

Be sure to write the formula as a part of an equation. For instance, do not just write $\dfrac{QL}{J}$ on your paper.

Rather, write $C = \dfrac{QL}{J}$. Look for language such as *is defined as* to identify what equals what.

Functions

Functions are very much like the "magic boxes" you may have learned about in elementary school.

> You put a 2 into the magic box, and a 7 comes out. You put a 3 into the magic box, and a 9 comes out. You put a 4 into the magic box, and an 11 comes out. What is the magic box doing to your number?

There are many possible ways to describe what the magic box is doing to your number. One possibility is as follows: The magic box is doubling your number and adding 3:

$$2(2) + 3 = 7 \qquad\qquad 2(3) + 3 = 9 \qquad\qquad 2(4) + 3 = 11$$

Assuming that this is the case (it is possible that the magic box is actually doing something different to your number), this description would yield the following rule for this magic box: $2x + 3$. This rule can be written in function form as:

$$f(x) = 2x + 3$$

The function f represents the rule that the magic box is using to transform your number.

The magic box analogy is a helpful way to conceptualize a function as a *rule* built on an independent variable. The value of a function changes as the value of the independent variable changes. In other words, the value of a function is dependent on the value of the independent variable. Examples of functions include:

$$f(x) = 4x^2 - 11 \qquad\qquad \text{The value of the function, } f, \text{ is dependent on the independent variable, } x.$$

$$g(t) = t^3 + \sqrt{t} - \frac{2t}{5} \qquad\qquad \text{The value of the function, } g, \text{ is dependent on the independent variable, } t.$$

You can think of functions as consisting of an *input* variable (the number you put into the magic box) and a corresponding *output* value (the number that comes out of the box). The function is the rule that turns the input variable into some output value.

By the way, the expression $f(x)$ is pronounced "*f* of *x*," not "*fx*." It does not mean "*f times x*"! The letter *f* does *not* stand for a variable; rather, it stands for the rule that dictates how the input *x* changes into the output $f(x)$.

The *domain* of a function indicates the possible inputs. The *range* of a function indicates the possible outputs. For instance, the function $f(x) = x^2$ can take any input but never produces a negative number. So the domain is all numbers, but the range is $f(x) \geq 0$.

The most basic type of function problem asks you to input the numerical value (say, 5) in place of the independent variable (x) to determine the value of the function.

> If $f(x) = x^2 - 2$, what is the value of $f(5)$?

In this problem, you are given a rule for $f(x)$: square x and subtract 2. Then, you are asked to apply this rule to the number 5. Square 5 and subtract 2 from the result:

$$f(5) = (5)^2 - 2 = 25 - 2 = 23$$

Variable Substitution in Functions

This type of function problem is slightly more complicated. Instead of finding the output value for a numerical input, you must find the output when the input is an algebraic expression.

> If $f(z) = z^2 - \dfrac{z}{3}$, what is the value of $f(3w + 6)$?

Input the variable expression $(3w + 6)$ in place of the independent variable (z) to determine the value of the function:

$$f(3w + 6) = (3w + 6)^2 - \frac{3w + 6}{3}$$

Compare this equation to the equation for $f(z)$. The expression $(3w + 6)$ has taken the place of every z in the original equation. In a sense, you are treating the expression $(3w + 6)$ as one thing, as if it were a single letter or variable.

The rest is algebraic simplification:

$$f(3w + 6) = (3w + 6)(3w + 6) - (w + 2)$$
$$= 9w^2 + 36w + 36 - w - 2$$
$$= 9w^2 + 35w + 34$$

Strange Symbol Formulas

Another type of GMAT formula problem involves the use of strange symbols. In these problems, the GMAT introduces an arbitrary symbol and uses it to define a certain procedure. People sometimes panic, thinking they forgot to study the weird symbol. Don't worry! The question will tell you what the symbol means.

It is helpful to break the operations down one by one and say them aloud (or in your head)—to "hear" them explicitly. Here are some examples:

Formula Definition	Step-by-Step Breakdown
$x \, \heartsuit \, y = x^2 + y^2 - xy$	"The first number squared, plus the second number squared, minus the product of the two…"
$s \circ t = (s - 2)(t + 2)$	"Subtract two from the first number, add two to the second number, then multiply them together…"
$\boxed{x}$ is defined as the product of all integers smaller than x but greater than 0…	"…x minus 1, times x minus 2, times x minus 3… Aha! So this is $(x - 1)$ factorial!"

Notice that it can be helpful to refer to the variables as "the first number," "the second number," and so on. In this way, you use the physical position of the numbers to keep them straight in relation to the strange symbol.

Now that you understand what the formula means, you can calculate a solution for the formula with actual numbers. Consider the following example:

$$W \, \psi \, F = \left(\sqrt{W}\right)^f \text{ for all integers } W \text{ and } F. \text{ What is } 4 \, \psi \, 5 \, ?$$

The symbol ψ between two numbers signals the following procedure: take the square root of the first number and then raise that value to the power of the second number.

$$4 \, \psi \, 5 = \left(\sqrt{4}\right)^5 = 2^5 = 32$$

Watch out for symbols that invert the order of an operation. It is easy to automatically translate the function in a left-to-right manner even when that is *not* what the function specifies.

$$W \, \Phi \, F = \left(\sqrt{F}\right)^W \text{ for all integers } W \text{ and } F. \text{ What is } 4 \, \Phi \, 9 \, ?$$

It would be easy to perform the first operation using W. However, notice that the order of the operation is *reversed*—you need to take the square root of the *second* number, raised to the power of the *first* number:

$$4 \, \Phi \, 9 = \left(\sqrt{9}\right)^4 = 3^4 = 81$$

More challenging strange-symbol problems require you to use the given procedure more than once. For example:

$$W \Phi F = \left(\sqrt{F}\right)^{W} \text{ for all integers } W \text{ and } F. \text{ What is } 2 \Phi (3 \Phi 16)?$$

Always perform the procedure inside the parentheses first:

$$3 \Phi 16 = \left(\sqrt{16}\right)^{3} = 4^{3} = 64$$

Now rewrite the original formula as follows: $2 \Phi (3 \Phi 16) = 2 \Phi 64$.

Performing the procedure a second time yields the answer:

$$2 \Phi 64 = \left(\sqrt{64}\right)^{2} = 8^{2} = 64$$

Squaring a square root will take you back to your starting point; if you notice this, you can cancel the two operations and you're left with 64.

Formulas That Act on Decimals

Occasionally, you might encounter a formula or special symbol that acts on decimals. Follow the formula's instructions *precisely*.

Define symbol $[x]$ to represent the largest integer less than or equal to x:

What is [5.1]?

According to the definition you are given, [5.1] is the largest integer less than or equal to 5.1. That integer is 5, so [5.1] = 5. Try another example:

What is [0.8]?

According to the definition again, [0.8] is the largest integer less than or equal to 0.8. That integer is 0. So [0.8] = 0. Notice that the result is *not* 1. This particular definition does not round the number. Rather, the operation *seems* to be truncation—simply cutting off the decimal. However, you must be careful with negatives. For example:

What is [−2.3]?

Once again, [−2.3] is the largest integer less than or equal to −2.3. Remember that "less than" on a number line means "to the left of." A "smaller" negative number is further away from 0 than a "bigger" negative number. So the largest integer less than −2.3 is −3, and [−2.3] = −3. Notice that the result is *not* −2; this bracket operation is *not* truncation.

Be sure to follow the instructions exactly whenever you are given a special symbol or formula involving decimals. It is easy to jump to conclusions about how an operation works; for instance, finding the largest integer less than x is *not* the same as rounding x or truncating x in all cases. Also, do not confuse this particular set of brackets $[x]$ with parentheses (x) or absolute value signs $|x|$.

Sequence Formulas

A sequence is a collection of numbers in a set order. Every sequence is defined by a rule, which you can use to find the values of terms:

$$A_n = 9n + 3$$

You can find the first term (A_1) by plugging $n = 1$ into the equation. $A_1 = 12$

You can find the second term (A_2) by plugging $n = 2$ into the equation. $A_2 = 21$

You can find the nth term (A_n) by plugging n into the equation.

If $S_n = 15n - 7$, what is the value of $S_7 - S_5$?

This question is asking for the difference between the seventh term and the fifth term of the sequence.

$$S_7 = 15(7) - 7 = 105 - 7 = 98$$

$$S_5 = 15(5) - 7 = 75 - 7 = 68$$

$$S_7 - S_5 = (98) - (68) = 30$$

Recursive Sequences

Occasionally, a sequence will be defined *recursively*. A recursive sequence defines each term relative to other terms. For example:

If $a_n = 2a_{n-1} - 4$, and $a_6 = -4$, what is the value of a_4?

If a_n represents the nth term, then a_{n-1} is the term right before a_n. You are given the value of the 6th term, and need to figure out the value of the 4th term. Keep track of this on your scrap paper.

$$\underbrace{\rule{3cm}{0.4pt}}_{a_4} \qquad \underbrace{\rule{3cm}{0.4pt}}_{a_5} \qquad \underbrace{\overset{-4}{\rule{3cm}{0.4pt}}}_{a_6}$$

Use the value of the sixth term (a_6) to find the value of the fifth term (a_5):

$$a_6 = 2a_5 - 4$$
$$(-4) = 2a_5 - 4$$
$$0 = 2a_5$$
$$0 = a_5$$

The value of the fifth term is 0:

$\underline{}$	$\underline{0}$	$\underline{-4}$
a_4	a_5	a_6

Now use the fifth term to find the fourth term:

$$a_5 = 2a_4 - 4$$
$$(0) = 2a_4 - 4$$
$$4 = 2a_4$$
$$2 = a_4$$

The value of the fourth term is 2.

When a sequence is defined recursively, the question will have to give you the value of at least one of the terms. Use that value to find the value of the desired term.

Linear Sequence Problems: Alternative Method

8

For linear sequences, in which the same number is added to any term to yield the next term, you can use the following alternative method:

> If each number in a sequence is 3 more than the previous number, and the 6th number is 32, what is the 100th number?

Instead of finding the rule for this sequence, consider the following reasoning: From the 6th to the 100th term, there are 94 "jumps" of 3. Since $94 \times 3 = 282$, there is an increase of 282 from the 6th term to the 100th term:

$$32 + 282 = 314$$

Problem Set

Now that you've finished the chapter, do the following problems.

For problems 1 and 2, use the following sequence: $A_n = 3 - 8n$.

1.   What is A_1?

2.   What is $A_{11} - A_9$?

3.   Given that $A \lozenge B = 4A - B$, what is the value of $(3 \lozenge 2) \lozenge 3$?

4.   Given that 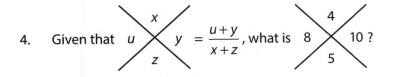 $= \dfrac{u+y}{x+z}$, what is $\begin{array}{c} 4 \\ 8 \quad\times\quad 10 \\ 5 \end{array}$?

5.   If $f(x) = 2x^4 - x^2$, what is the value of $f(2\sqrt{3})$?

6.   If $a_n = \dfrac{a_{n-1} \times a_{n-2}}{2}$, $a_5 = -6$, and $a_6 = -18$, what is the value of a_3?

Save the below problem set for review, either after you finish this book or after you finish all of the Quant books that you plan to study.

7.   Life expectancy is defined by the formula $\dfrac{2SB}{G}$, where S = shoe size, B = average monthly electric bill in dollars, and G = GMAT score. If Melvin's GMAT score is twice his monthly electric bill, and his life expectancy is 50, what is his shoe size?

8.   The "competitive edge" of a baseball team is defined by the formula $\sqrt{\dfrac{W}{L}}$, where W represents the number of the team's wins and L represents the number of the team's losses. This year, the GMAT All-Stars had 3 times as many wins and one-half as many losses as they had last year. By what factor did their "competitive edge" increase?

9.   If $k(x) = 4x^3a$, and $k(3) = 27$, what is $k(2)$?

10.   The first term in an arithmetic sequence is −5 and the second term is −3. What is the 50th term? (Recall that in an arithmetic sequence, the difference between successive terms is constant.)

11.   Given that $\begin{array}{|c|} \hline A \\ B \\ \hline \end{array} = A^2 + B^2 + 2AB$, what is $A + B$, if $\begin{array}{|c|} \hline A \\ B \\ \hline \end{array} = 9$?

12.   If $f(x) = 2x^2 - 4$ and $g(x) = 2x$, for what values of x will $f(x) = g(x)$?

8

Solutions

1. –5: $A_n = 3 - 8n$

$A_1 = 3 - 8(1) = 3 - 8 = -5$

2. –16: $A_n = 3 - 8n$

$A_{11} = 3 - 8(11) = 3 - 88 = -85$

$A_9 = 3 - 8(9) = 3 - 72 = -69$

$A_{11} - A_9 = -85 - (-69) = -16$

3. 37: First, simplify $3 \lozenge 2$: $4(3) - 2 = 12 - 2 = 10$. Then, solve $10 \lozenge 3$: $4(10) - 3 = 40 - 3 = 37$.

4. 2: Plug the numbers in the grid into the formula, matching up the number in each section with the corresponding variable in the formula: $\dfrac{u+y}{x+z} = \dfrac{8+10}{4+5} = \dfrac{18}{9} = 2$.

5. 276:

$$f(x) = 2\left(2\sqrt{3}\right)^4 - \left(2\sqrt{3}\right)^2$$
$$= 2(2)^4\left(\sqrt{3}\right)^4 - (2)^2\left(\sqrt{3}\right)^2$$
$$= (2 \times 16 \times 9) - (4 \times 3)$$
$$= 288 - 12 = 276$$

6. –2: According to the formula, $a_3 = \dfrac{a_2 \times a_1}{2}$. But you aren't given a_1 or a_2. Instead, you're given a_5 and a_6. You have to work backwards from the fifth and sixth terms of the sequence to find the third term. Notice what happens if you plug $n = 6$ into the formula:

$$a_6 = \frac{a_5 \times a_4}{2}$$

If you plug in the values of a_5 and a_6, you can solve for the value of a_4:

$$-18 = \frac{-6 \times a_4}{2}$$
$$-36 = -6 \times a_4$$
$$6 = a_4$$

8

Now you can use the fourth and fifth terms of the sequence to solve for a_3:

$$a_5 = \frac{a_4 \times a_3}{2}$$

$$-6 = \frac{6 \times a_3}{2}$$

$$-12 = 6 \times a_3$$

$$-2 = a_3$$

7. **Size 50:** Substitute $2B$ for G in the formula. Note that the term $2B$ appears in both the numerator and denominator, so they cancel out.

$$\frac{2SB}{2B} = 50$$

$$S = 50$$

8. $\sqrt{6}$: Let c = competitive edge:

$$c = \sqrt{\frac{W}{L}}$$

Pick numbers to see what happens to the competitive edge when W is tripled and L is halved. If the original value of W is 4 and the original value of L is 2, the original value of c is $\sqrt{\frac{4}{2}} = \sqrt{2}$. If W triples to 12 and L is halved to 1, the new value of c is $\sqrt{\frac{12}{1}} = \sqrt{12}$. The competitive edge has increased from $\sqrt{2}$ to $\sqrt{12}$. Therefore:

$$\frac{\sqrt{12}}{\sqrt{2}} = \sqrt{\frac{12}{2}} = \sqrt{6}$$

The competitive edge has increased by a factor of $\sqrt{6}$.

9. **8:** If $k(3) = 27$, then you know the following:

$$4(3)^3 a = 27 \qquad\qquad k(x) = 4x^3\left(\frac{1}{4}\right) = x^3 \qquad\longrightarrow\qquad k(2) = (2)^3 = 8$$

$$4(27)a = 27$$

$$4a = 1$$

$$a = \frac{1}{4}$$

10. **93:** The first term is −5 and the second term is −3, so you are adding +2 to each successive term. How many times do you have to add 2? There are $50 − 1 = 49$ additional "steps" after the 1st term, so you have to add +2 a total of 49 times, beginning with your starting point of −5: $−5 + 2(49) = 93$.

11. **{3, −3}:** First, set the formula equal to 9. Then, factor the expression $A^2 + B^2 + 2AB$. Unsquare both sides, taking both the positive and negative roots into account.

$$A^2 + B^2 + 2AB = 9$$
$$(A + B)^2 = 9$$

$$A + B = 3 \qquad OR \qquad A + B = −3$$

12. **{−1, 2}:** To find the values for which $f(x) = g(x)$, set the functions equal to each other:

$$2x^2 − 4 = 2x$$
$$2x^2 − 2x − 4 = 0$$
$$2(x^2 − x − 2) = 0$$
$$2(x − 2)(x + 1) = 0$$

$$x − 2 = 0 \qquad OR \qquad x + 1 = 0$$
$$x = 2 \qquad\qquad\qquad x = −1$$

8

Chapter 9 *of* Algebra

Inequalities

In This Chapter. . .

Chapter 9
Inequalities

Unlike equations, which relate two equivalent quantities, inequalities compare quantities that have different values. Inequalities are used to express four kinds of relationships, illustrated by the following examples.

1. x is less than 4

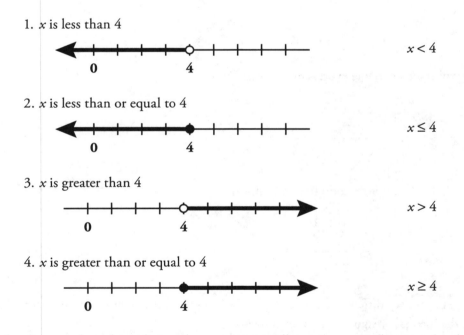

$x < 4$

2. x is less than or equal to 4

$x \leq 4$

3. x is greater than 4

$x > 4$

4. x is greater than or equal to 4

$x \geq 4$

Number lines, such as those shown above, are an excellent way to visualize exactly what a given inequality means.

When you see inequalities with 0 on one side of the inequality, consider using positive/negative analysis to help solve the problem!

Here are some common inequality statements on the GMAT, as well as what they imply.

STATEMENT	IMPLICATION
$xy > 0$	x and y are *both positive* OR *both negative*
$xy < 0$	x and y have *different signs* (one positive, one negative)
$x^2 - x < 0$	$x^2 < x$, so $0 < x < 1$

Flip the Sign

Most operations that can be performed on equations can be performed on inequalities. For example, in order to simplify an inequality (e.g., $2 + x < 5$), you can add or subtract a constant on both sides:

$$\begin{array}{ll} 2 + x < 5 \\ \underline{-2 \qquad -2} \\ \qquad x < 3 \end{array} \qquad \begin{array}{ll} x - 5 < 9 \\ \underline{+5 \quad +5} \\ x \qquad < 14 \end{array}$$

You can also add or subtract a variable expression on both sides:

$$\begin{array}{ll} y + x < 5 \\ \underline{-y \qquad -y} \\ \qquad x < 5 - y \end{array} \qquad \begin{array}{ll} x - ab < 9 \\ \underline{+ab \quad +ab} \\ x \qquad < 9 + ab \end{array}$$

You can multiply or divide by a *positive* number on both sides:

$$\begin{array}{ll} 2x < 6 \\ \underline{\div 2 \quad \div 2} \\ \quad x < 3 \end{array} \qquad \begin{array}{ll} 0.2x < 1 \\ \underline{\times 5 \quad \times 5} \\ \quad x < 5 \end{array}$$

One procedure, however, is very different for inequalities: When you multiply or divide an inequality by a negative number, the inequality sign flips! For example:

Given that $4 - 3x < 10$, what is the range of possible values for x?

$$\begin{array}{ll} 4 - 3x < 10 \\ \underline{-4 \qquad -4} \\ \quad -3x < 6 \\ \underline{\div(-3) \ \div(-3)} \\ \qquad x > -2 \end{array}$$

First, subtract 4 from both sides.

Next, divide by -3. Because you're dividing by a negative, flip the inequality sign.

MANHATTAN
PREP

Do not multiply or divide an inequality by a variable unless you know the sign of the number that the variable stands for. If you don't know whether that number is positive or negative, then you don't know whether to flip the inequality sign.

Combining Inequalities: Line 'Em Up!

Many GMAT inequality problems involve more than one inequality. To solve such problems, you may need to convert several inequalities to a compound inequality, which is a series of inequalities strung together, such as $2 < 3 < 4$. To convert multiple inequalities to a compound inequality, first line up the variables, then combine.

> If $x > 8$, $x < 17$, and $x + 5 < 19$, what is the range of possible values for x?

First, solve any inequalities that need to be solved. In this example, only the last inequality needs to be solved:

$$x + 5 < 19$$
$$x < 14$$

Second, simplify the inequalities so that all the inequality symbols point in the same direction, and then line up the common variables in the inequalities:

$$8 < x$$
$$x < 17$$
$$x < 14$$

Finally, put the information together. Notice that $x < 14$ is more limiting than $x < 17$ (in other words, whenever $x < 14$, x will always be less than 17, but not vice versa.) The range, then, is $8 < x < 14$ rather than $8 < x < 17$. Discard the less limiting inequality, $x < 17$. Try another example:

> Given that $u < t$, $b > r$, $f < t$, and $r > t$, is $b > u$?

Combine the four given inequalities by simplifying and lining up the common variables.

Align all inequalities in the same direction: $u < t$, $r < b$, $f < t$, and $t < r$.

Then, line up the variables...   ...and combine.

$$u < t$$ $$u < t < r < b$$
$$\quad\quad r < b$$ $$f < t < r < b$$
$$f < t$$
$$\quad t < r$$

It is not always possible to combine all the information into a single compound inequality, as you see in this example. You know that both *u* and *f* are less than *t*, but you do not know the relationship between *u* and *f*.

The answer to the question is yes, *b* is greater than *u*.

Manipulating Compound Inequalities

Sometimes a problem with compound inequalities will require you to manipulate the inequalities in order to solve the problem. You can perform operations on a compound inequality as long as you remember to perform those operations on every term in the inequality, not just the outside terms. For example:

$x + 3 < y < x + 5 \not\rightarrow x < y < x + 2$ **WRONG**: You must subtract 3 from *every* term in the inequality

$x + 3 < y < x + 5 \rightarrow x < y - 3 < x + 2$ CORRECT

$\dfrac{c}{2} \le b - 3 \le \dfrac{d}{2} \rightarrow c \le b - 3 \le d$ **WRONG**: You must multiply by 2 in *every* term in the inequality

$\dfrac{c}{2} \le b - 3 \le \dfrac{d}{2} \rightarrow c \le 2b - 6 \le d$ CORRECT

If $1 > 1 - ab > 0$, which of the following must be true?

    I. $\dfrac{a}{b} > 0$

    II. $\dfrac{a}{b} < 1$

    III. $ab < 1$

(A) I only
(B) II only
(C) III only
(D) I and II only
(E) I and III only

You can manipulate the original compound inequality as follows, making sure to perform each manipulation on every term:

$1 > 1 - ab > 0$
$0 > \quad -ab > -1$ Subtract 1 from all three terms.
$0 < \quad\quad ab < 1$ Multiply all three terms by −1 and flip the inequality signs.

Therefore, you know that $0 < ab < 1$. This tells you that ab is positive, so $\dfrac{a}{b}$ must be positive (a and b have the same sign). Therefore, statement I must be true. However, you do not know whether $\dfrac{a}{b} < 1$, so statement II is not necessarily true. But you do know that ab must be less than 1, so statement III must be true. Therefore, the correct answer is **(E)**.

Combining Inequalities: Add 'Em Up!

You can combine inequalities by adding the inequalities together. In order to add inequalities, the inequality signs must face in the same direction.

> Is $a + 2b < c + 2d$?
>
> > (1) $a < c$
> > (2) $d > b$

Assume that you've already tried the two statements individually and neither was sufficient by itself. In order to test the statements together, add the inequalities together to see whether they match the question. First, line up the inequalities so that they are all facing the same direction:

$$a < c$$
$$b < d$$

Then, take the sum of the two inequalities to prove the result. You will need to add the second inequality *twice*:

$$
\begin{array}{r}
a < c \\
+\quad b < d \\
\hline
a + b < c + d \\
+\quad b < d \\
\hline
a + 2b < c + 2d
\end{array}
$$

If you use both statements, you can answer the question. Therefore, the answer is **(C)**.

Notice that you also could have multiplied the second inequality by 2 before summing, so that the result matched the original question:

$$a \qquad < c$$
$$+ \quad \underline{2(b < \qquad d)}$$
$$a + 2b < c + 2d$$

Adding inequalities together is a powerful technique on the GMAT. However, never subtract or divide two inequalities. You can multiply inequalities together as long as all possible values of the inequalities are positive, but the GMAT rarely tests this skill.

Square-Rooting Inequalities

Just like equations involving even exponents, inequality problems involving even exponents require you to consider *two* scenarios. Consider this example:

If $x^2 < 4$, what are the possible values for x?

To solve this problem, recall that $\sqrt{x^2} = |x|$. For example, $\sqrt{3^2} = 3$ and $\sqrt{(-5)^2} = 5$. Therefore, when you take the square root of both sides of the inequality, you get:

$$\sqrt{x^2} < \sqrt{4}$$
$$|x| < 2$$

If x is positive, then $x < 2$. On the other hand, if x is negative, then $x > -2$.

Here is another example:

If $10 + x^2 \geq 19$, what is the range of possible values for x?

$$10 + x^2 \geq 19$$
$$x^2 \geq 9$$
$$|x| \geq 3$$

If x is positive, then $x \geq 3$. If x is negative, then $x \leq -3$.

Note that you can *only* take the square root of an inequality for which both sides are definitely *not* negative, since you cannot take the square root of a negative number. Restrict this technique to situations in which the square of a variable or expression must be positive.

Problem Set

Now that you've finished the chapter, do the following problems.

1. Which of the following is equivalent to $-3x + 7 \le 2x + 32$?

    (A) $x \ge -5$ (B) $x \ge 5$ (C) $x \le 5$ (D) $x \le -5$

2. If $G^2 < G$, which of the following could be G?

    (A) 1   (B) $\dfrac{23}{7}$ (C) $\dfrac{7}{23}$ (D) -4 (E) -2

3. If $5B > 4B + 1$, is $B^2 > 1$?

4. If $|A| > 19$, which of the following could not be equal to A?

    (A) 26   (B) 22   (C) 18   (D) -20 (E) -24

5. If $|10y - 4| > 7$ and $y < 1$, which of the following could be y?

    (A) -0.8 (B) -0.1 (C) 0.1   (D) 0   (E) 1

6. A retailer sells only radios and clocks. If she currently has 44 total items in inventory, how many of them are radios?

    (1) The retailer has more than 28 radios in inventory.
    (2) The retailer has less than twice as many radios as clocks in inventory.

Save the below problem set for review, either after you finish this book or after you finish all of the Quant books that you plan to study.

7. If $a > 7$, $a + 4 > 13$, and $2a < 30$, which of the following must be true?

    (A) $9 < a < 15$ (B) $11 < a < 15$ (C) $15 < a < 20$ (D) $13 < a < 15$

8. If $d > a$ and $L < a$, which of the following cannot be true?

    (A) $d + L = 14$ (B) $d - L = 7$ (C) $d - L = 1$ (D) $a - d = 9$ (E) $a + d = 9$

9. If $\dfrac{AB}{7} > \dfrac{1}{14}$ and $A = B$, which of the following must be greater than 1?

    (A) $A + B$ (B) $1 - A$ (C) $2A^2$ (D) $A^2 - \dfrac{1}{2}$ (E) A

10. If $4x - 12 \geq x + 9$, which of the following must be true?

   (A) $x > 6$ (B) $x < 7$ (C) $x > 7$ (D) $x > 8$ (E) $x < 8$

11. If $0 < ab < ac$, is a negative?

   (1) $c < 0$
   (2) $b > c$

12. Eco Wildlife Preserve contains $5x$ zebras and $2x$ lions, where x is a positive integer. If the lions succeed in killing z of the zebras, is the new ratio of zebras to lions less than 2 to 1?

   (1) $z > x$
   (2) $z = 4$

Solutions

1. (A): $-3x + 7 \leq 2x + 32$
$\qquad -5x \leq 25$
$\qquad x \geq -5$

2. (C): If $G^2 < G$, then G must be positive (since G^2 will never be negative), and G must be less than 1, because otherwise $G^2 > G$. Thus, $0 < G < 1$. You can eliminate (D) and (E), since they violate the condition that G be positive. Then test (A): 1 is not less than 1, so you can eliminate (A). (B) is larger than 1, so only (C) satisfies the inequality.

3. YES: $5B > 4B + 1$
$\qquad B > 1$

The squares of all numbers greater than 1 are also greater than 1, so $B^2 > 1$.

4. (C): If $|A| > 19$, then $A > 19$ OR $A < -19$. The only answer choice that does not satisfy either of these inequalities is (C), 18.

5. (A): First, eliminate any answer choices that do not satisfy the simpler of the two inequalities, $y < 1$. Based on this inequality alone, you can eliminate (E). Then, simplify the first inequality:

$$10y - 4 > 7 \qquad \text{OR} \qquad -10y + 4 > 7$$
$$10y > 11 \qquad\qquad\qquad 10y < -3$$
$$y > 1.1 \qquad\qquad\qquad y < -\frac{3}{10}$$

The only answer choice that satisfies this inequality is (A), -0.8.

6. (C): First assign r equal to the number of radios the retailer has in inventory and c equal to the number of clocks the retailer has in inventory. You can translate the information in the question stem:

$$r + c = 44$$

The question now becomes: What is r?

(1) INSUFFICIENT: This only tells you that $r \geq 29$. r could equal 29, 30, 40, etc.

(2) INSUFFICIENT: This only tells you that $r < 2c$. Combining this information with the original equation from the problem gives you:

$$r < 2c$$
$$r + c = 44$$

If you isolate c in the second equation, you can then substitute into the inequality:

$$c = 44 - r$$

$$r < 2c$$
$$r < 2(44 - r)$$
$$r < 88 - 2r$$
$$3r < 88$$
$$r < \frac{88}{3}$$

Thus, $\frac{88}{3}$ is equal to $29\frac{1}{3}$. Therefore, you know that r must be less than or equal to 29 (because r must be an integer). This information on its own, however, is insufficient.

(1) AND (2) SUFFICIENT: Statement (1) tells you $r \geq 29$ and statement (2) tells you $r \leq 29$. Therefore, r must equal 29.

The correct answer is **(C)**.

7. **(A):** First, solve the second and third inequalities. Simplify the inequalities, so that all the inequality symbols point in the same direction. Then, line up the inequalities as shown. Finally, combine the inequalities:

$$9 < a$$
$$a < 15 \quad \longrightarrow \quad 9 < a < 15$$
$$7 < a$$

Notice that all the wrong answers are more constrained: the low end is too high. The right answer will both keep out all the impossible values of a *and* let in all the possible values of a.

8. **(D):** Simplify the inequalities, so that all the inequality symbols point in the same direction. Then, line up the inequalities as shown. Finally, combine the inequalities:

$$L < a$$
$$a < d \quad \longrightarrow \quad L < a < d$$

Since d is a larger number than a, $a - d$ cannot be positive. Therefore, (D) cannot be true.

9. **(C):** $\dfrac{AB}{7} > \dfrac{1}{14}$

$14AB > 7$	Cross-multiply across the inequality.
$2AB > 1$	Divide both sides by 7.
$2A^2 > 1$	Since you know that $A = B$, then $2AB = 2A^2$.

Note that you need to get the expression > 1 on the right because the question asked what must be greater than 1.

10. **(A):** $4x - 12 \geq x + 9$

$\qquad 3x \geq 21$

$\qquad\quad x \geq 7$

You were asked to pick the answer that *must be* true. If x is greater than or equal to 7, then x could be 7, 7.3, 8, 9.2, and so on. Which of the five answers contains an expression that covers all possible values of x? Most people will immediately look at answer (C) $x > 7$, but be careful! Does x have to be greater than 7? No; x could be 7 itself, in which case answer (C) is inaccurate. Similarly, answers (D) and (E) cover some of the possible values for x, but not *all* of them. Answer (B) doesn't share anything in common with $x > 7$, so it's wrong. You're left with answer (A). Why must it be true that x is greater than 6? Because x could be 7, 7.3, 8, 9.2, and so on. All of those possible values for x are greater than 6. The logic here is very similar to that of Data Sufficiency: if $x \geq 7$ were a statement, it would be sufficient to establish that $x > 6$.

11. **(D):** By the transitive property of inequalities, if $0 < ab < ac$, then $0 < ac$. Therefore, a and c must have the same sign.

(1) SUFFICIENT: Statement (1) tells you that c is negative. Therefore, a is negative.

(2) SUFFICIENT: Statement (2) is trickier. The statement indicates that $b > c$, but the question stem also told you that $ab < ac$. When you multiply both sides of $b > c$ by a, the sign gets flipped. For inequalities, what circumstance needs to be true in order to flip the sign when you multiply by something? You multiply by a negative. Therefore, a must be negative, because multiplying the two sides of the equation by a results in a flipped inequality sign.

The correct answer is (D).

12. **(A):** The ratio of zebras to lions can be written as $\dfrac{5x}{2x}$.

If z zebras then meet a sad ending, the new ratio can be written as $\dfrac{5x - z}{2x}$.

(Note that it's fine to "mix" the ratio with the variable z, since the ratio itself already contains the variable x, which is the multiplier — that is, x is the number you would multiply 5 and 2 by to get the real, original numbers of zebras and lions.

Thus, you can rephrase the question as:

$$\dfrac{5x - z}{2x} < \dfrac{2}{1}?$$

But you can keep simplifying! (If the DS question contains fractions, or the same variable in more than one place, try to simplify a bit more.) Since you know that x is positive, you can cross-multiply:

$$5x - z < 4x?$$
$$-z < -x?$$
$$z > x?$$

The question is asking, "Is $z > x$?"

(1) SUFFICIENT: This statement answers the rephrased question directly.

Alternatively, plugging in values for z and x would also show the statement to be sufficient if you didn't take the algebraic route. For instance, if $z = 3$ and $x = 2$, then you would start with 10 zebras and 4 lions, and then losing three zebras would give you 7 zebras to 4 lions, which is less than a 2 to 1 ratio. Additional examples will yield the same results.

(2) INSUFFICIENT: Knowing that $z = 4$ is not sufficient without knowing something about x. For instance, if $x = 1$ and you began with 5 zebras and 2 lions, then losing 4 zebras would certainly shift the ratio below 2 to 1. But what if x were 100? If you began with 500 zebras and 200 lions, then the loss of 4 zebras would not shift the ratio below 2 to 1.

The correct answer is (A).

Chapter 10

of

Algebra

Strategy: Test Cases

In This Chapter...

Chapter 10

Strategy: Test Cases

Certain problems allow for multiple possible scenarios, or cases. When you **Test Cases,** you try different numbers in a problem to see whether you have the same outcome or different outcomes.

The strategy plays out a bit differently for Data Sufficiency (DS) versus Problem Solving. This chapter will focus on DS problems; if you have not yet studied DS, please see Appendix A of this guide. For a full treatment of Problem Solving, see the Test Cases strategy chapter in the *Number Properties GMAT Strategy Guide*.

Try this problem, using any solution method you like:

Is $m < n$?

(1) $m < n^2$
(2) $|m| < n$

How to Test Cases

Here's how to test cases to solve the above problem.

Step 1: Set up the base scenario: what possible cases are allowed?

The problem asks about the variables m and n but does not give any constraints. (A constraint, for example, might be, "If m and n are integers …," in which case you are only allowed to try integers for the two variables.)

Step 2: Remind yourself: choose numbers that make the statement true.

Before you dive into the work, remember this crucial rule:

Tip: When choosing numbers to Test Cases, ONLY choose numbers that make the statement true.

If you inadvertently choose numbers that make the statement false, discard that case and try again.

Step 3: Try to prove the statement *Insufficient*.

Here's how:

> (1) $m < n^2$

What numbers would make this statement true?

> Case 1: $m = 1$, $n = 2$

Statement True? ($m < n^2$)	Is $m < n$?
$1 < 4$ ✓	Yes

First, ensure that the value you've chosen to test does make the statement true. In this case, m is indeed smaller than n^2.

Second, answer the question asked. If $m = 1$ and $n = 2$, then Yes, $m < n$.

Next, ask yourself: Is there another possible case that would give you a *different* outcome?

> Case 2: $m = 1$, $n = -2$

Statement True? ($m < n^2$)	Is $m < n$?
$1 < 4$ ✓	No

Because the answer is Sometimes Yes, Sometimes No, this statement is not sufficient; cross off answers (A) and (D). Try statement (2) next.

~~AD~~
BCE

> (2) $|m| < n$

Case 1: $m = 1$, $n = 2$

Statement True? ($|m| < n$)	Is $m < n$?
$1 < 2$ ✓	Yes

Is there another possible case that would give you a different outcome?

Case 2: $m = 1$, $n = -2$

Statement True? ($|m| < n$)	Is $m < n$?
$1 < -2$ ✗	

Careful! This time, the numbers don't work. You are required to pick values that make statement (2) true. Discard this case. (Literally cross it off on your scrap paper.)

What else might give a No outcome?

Case 3: $m = -2$, $n = -2$

Statement True? ($|m| < n$)	Is $m < n$?
$2 < -2$ ✗	

Nope, they can't both be negative either, nor can they equal each other.

It turns out that, no matter how many cases you try for statement (2), you are always going to get a Yes outcome. In other words, the only cases that will make the statement true are those that return a Yes outcome to the question. Why?

Taking the absolute value of m turns that number positive or keeps it 0 (if $m = 0$). If $|m| < n$, then n has to be positive. Further, n has to be greater than the positive version of m, in order for the statement to be true. This statement is sufficient.

The correct answer is (**B**).   ~~AD~~
                                  (B)CE

When you test cases in Data Sufficiency, your ultimate goal is to try to prove the statement insufficient, if you can. The first case you try will give you one outcome. For the next case, think about numbers that would be likely to give a *different* outcome.

As soon as you do find two different outcomes, as in statement (1) above, you know the statement is not sufficient, and you can cross off some answer choices and move on.

If you cannot find two different outcomes, then you may be able to prove to yourself why you will always get the same outcome, as in statement (2) above. If you have tried several times to prove the statement insufficient but you keep getting the same outcome, then that statement probably is sufficient.

Try another one:

Is $d > 0$?

(1) $bc < 0$
(2) $cd > 0$

Step 1: Set up the base scenario: what possible cases are allowed?

The question stem does not provide any constraints, so think about trying negatives or fractions, where appropriate.

Step 2: Remind yourself: choose numbers that make the statement true.

Separate your evaluation into two parts: first, have you chosen numbers that make this statement true? Second, is the outcome to the question Yes or No based on this one case?

Step 3: Try to prove the statement *insufficient*.

(1) $bc < 0$

At the most basic level, this statement cannot be sufficient because it mentions nothing about d. It does, though, tell you one piece of info: if b and c multiply to a negative number, then b and c must have opposite signs. File that piece of information away for later, just in case.

Also, note that this approach used number theory to analyze the problem. Trying real numbers to figure out this theory would also work.

This statement is not sufficient to answer the question. Cross off answers (A) and (D).
~~AD~~
BCE

(2) $cd > 0$

If c and d multiply to a positive number, then c and d must have the same sign: both positive or both negative.

In this case, d could be positive or negative, so this statement is not sufficient to answer the question. Cross off (B) and try the two statements together:
~~AD~~
~~B~~CE

(1) $bc < 0$
(2) $cd > 0$

Map out the scenarios to make sure that you correctly keep track of it all. If b is positive, then c has to be negative. In that case, d also has to be negative:

b	c	d	$bc < 0$?	$cd > 0$?	$d > 0$?
+	−	−	✓	✓	No
−	+	+	✓	✓	Yes

If b is negative, however, then c has to be positive. In that case, d also has to be positive.

A Sometimes Yes, Sometimes No answer is not sufficient. The correct answer is (E).
~~AD~~
~~B~~ ~~C~~(E)

You can test cases by using real numbers or by thinking through the math theoretically, whatever you find best for a particular problem. In general, when you really understand the theory, that path will be fastest. If you are at all unsure about the theory, then it's best to test real numbers.

In sum, when you have decided to test cases, follow three main steps:

Step 1: What possible cases are allowed?

Before you start solving, make sure you know what restrictions have been placed on the basic problem in the question stem. You may be told that the number is an integer, or positive, or odd, and so on. Follow these restrictions when choosing numbers to try later in your work.

Step 2: Choose numbers that make the statement true.

Pause for a moment to remind yourself that you are only allowed to choose numbers for each statement that make that particular statement true. With enough practice, this will begin to become second nature. If you answer a testing cases problem incorrectly but aren't sure why, see whether you accidentally tested cases that weren't allowed because they didn't make the statement true.

Step 3: Try to prove the statement *insufficient*.

Value

> Sufficient: single numerical answer
> Not Sufficient: two or more possible answers

Yes/No

> Sufficient: Always Yes *or* Always No
> Not Sufficient: Maybe or Sometimes Yes, Sometimes No

When to Test Cases

You can test cases whenever the statements of a DS problem allow multiple possible starting points or scenarios that fulfill the conditions. In that case, try some of the different possibilities allowed in order to see whether these different scenarios, or cases, result in different answers or in the same answer to the question.

When testing cases, your initial starting point is every possible number on the number line. However, many problems give you restrictions that narrow the possible values, such as specifying that a number has to be an integer, or less than 0, or even. Write down your restrictions before you begin testing cases.

Think about different classes of numbers that are commonly tested on the GMAT. For example:

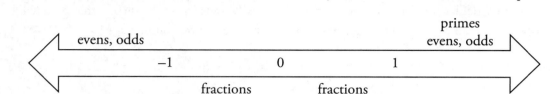

Try the following problem:

Is $b < 0$?

(1) $b^3 < b$
(2) $b^2 > b$

Step 1: What possible cases are allowed?

The question stem does not restrict the possible values for b.

Step 2: Choose numbers that make the statement true.

Step 3: Try to prove the statement *insufficient*.

(1) $b^3 < b$

Case 1: If $b = \dfrac{1}{2}$, then $\dfrac{1}{8} < \dfrac{1}{2}$. Therefore, $\dfrac{1}{2}$ is a possible value for b. In this case, no, b is not less than 0.

Case 2: If $b = 1$, then it is not true that $1 < 1$. Discard this case. Any number greater than 1 will not make this statement true.

Case 3: If $b = -2$, then $-8 < -2$. Therefore, -2 is a possible value for b. In this case, yes, b is less than 0.

This statement is insufficient; eliminate answers (A) and (D). Now look at statement (2):

~~AD~~
BCE

(2) $b^2 > b$

What numbers make this statement true?

Case 1: If $b = 2$, then $4 > 2$. Therefore, 2 is a possible value and, in this case, no, b is not less than 0.

Case 2: If $b = \dfrac{1}{2}$, then it is not true that $\dfrac{1}{4} > \dfrac{1}{2}$. Discard this case.

Case 3: If $b = -2$, then $4 > -2$. Therefore, -2 is a possible value and, in this case, yes, b is less than 0.

Statement (2) is also insufficient; eliminate answer (B).   A̶D̶

B̶CE

Try the two statements together:

(1) $b^3 < b$
(2) $b^2 > b$

Statement (1) allows b to be a fraction between 0 and 1 or a negative number smaller than -1.
Statement (2) allows b to be a positive number greater than 1 or any negative number.

The two statements only overlap for negative numbers smaller than -1. As a result, b must be a negative number. Together, the statements are sufficient.

The correct answer is (C).   A̶D̶

B̶©E

How to Get Better at Testing Cases

Practice makes perfect. First, try the problems at the end of this chapter using the three-step process detailed above. If you mess up any part of the process, try the problem again, making sure to write out all of your work.

Afterwards, review the problem. In particular, see whether you can articulate the reason why certain statements are sufficient (as the solutions to the earlier problems did). Could you explain to a fellow student who is confused? If so, then you are starting to learn both the process by which you test cases and the underlying principles that these kinds of problems test.

Next, try some problems from the online *Official Guide* problem sets. Again, review your work afterward. If you have any difficulties, look up the solution in the GMAT Navigator™ program, search online, or ask an instructor or fellow student for help.

10

Problem Set

It's time to practice your testing cases skills.

1. If $y > 0$, what is the value of y?

    (1) $y^2 \leq y$
    (2) y is an integer.

2. If n is a one-digit positive integer, what is n?

    (1) The units digit of 4^n is 4.
    (2) The units digit of n^4 is n.

3. Is $z > 0$?

    (1) $(z + 1)(z)(z - 1) < 0$
    (2) $|z| < 1$

Solutions

1. **(C):** The question stem allows any positive values for *y*, including fractions. The second statement is considerably easier than the first, so you might choose to start there.

(2) INSUFFICIENT: The statement indicates that *y* is an integer. The value of *y* could be 1, 2, 14, 192, or any other positive integer.

(1) INSUFFICIENT: What numbers make $y^2 \leq y$ true?

> Case 1: If $y = 1$, then $1 \leq 1$. Therefore, 1 is a possible value for *y*.

> Case 2: If $y = \dfrac{1}{2}$, then $\dfrac{1}{4} \leq \dfrac{1}{2}$. Therefore, $\dfrac{1}{2}$ is a possible value for *y*.

There are at least two possible values for *y*.

(1) AND (2) SUFFICIENT: Together, the two statements eliminate the fraction case $y = \dfrac{1}{2}$, but $y = 1$ is still a valid case. In order for $y^2 \leq y$ to be true, *y* must equal 0, 1, or a fraction between 0 and 1. If *y* is a positive integer, then it cannot be 0 or a fraction. The two statements together, then, are sufficient to answer the question: the value of *y* is 1.

The correct answer is (C).

2. **(E):** If *n* is a one-digit positive integer, it has to be 1, 2, 3, 4, 5, 6, 7, 8, or 9.

(1) INSUFFICIENT: The units digit of 4^n is 4.

Case	*n*	The units digit of 4^n is 4.	What is *n*?
#1	1	$4^1 = 4$ ✓	1
#2	2	$4^2 = 16$ ✗	
#3	3	$4^3 = 64$ ✓	3

Since *n* could be 1 or 3, statement (1) is not sufficient. (You might notice a pattern. It turns out that every *n* = odd will return a units digit of 4. Every *n* = even will return a units digit of 6.)

(2) INSUFFICIENT: The units digit of n^4 is *n*.

Case	*n*	The units digit of n^4 is *n*.	What is *n*?
#1	1	$1^4 = 1$ ✓	1
#2	2	$2^4 = 16$ ✗	
#3	3	$3^4 = 81$ ✗	

You can continue to test each possible value for *n* in order, or you can think about any patterns you know for raising a number to a power.

For example, raising 5 to any power will always return a number that ends in 5. Therefore 5^4 will end in 5, so 5 is a valid number for *n*.

n	The units digit of n^4 is *n*.	What is *n*?
5	$5^4 = 625$ ✓	5

Because there are at least two possible values for *n*, statement (2) is not sufficient.

(1) AND (2) INSUFFICIENT: Both statements allow *n* = 1. Statement (2) does not allow 3, but does allow 5. Does *n* = 5 work for the first statement?

n	The units digit of 4^n is 4.	What is *n*?
5	$4^5 =$ (ends in 4) ✓	4

Note that you do *not* actually multiply out 4^5. Instead, note the pattern:

4^n	Units digit
4^1	4
4^2	6
4^3	4
4^4	6

This pattern repeats to infinity.

Because both 1 and 5 work for each statement, even the two statements together are not sufficient to answer the question.

The correct answer is (E).

3. **(C):** This is a tough one. The question stem asks whether *z* is positive. Both statements look fairly complicated, so start with whichever one looks better to you.

(1) INSUFFICIENT: Many people will try *z* = 0, 1, or 2 first. All of these cases are invalid (0 and 1 return a product of 0, which is not *less* than 0, and 2 returns a positive product). Even −1 doesn't work! Think outside of the box: what weirder numbers can you try?

Case	*z*	$(z+1)(z)(z-1) < 0$	Is *z* > 0?
#1	−2	$(-1)(-2)(-3) = -6$ ✓	No
#2	$\dfrac{1}{2}$	$\left(\dfrac{3}{2}\right)\left(\dfrac{1}{2}\right)\left(-\dfrac{1}{2}\right) = -\dfrac{3}{8}$ ✓	Yes

Careful! While the three terms *z* + 1, *z*, and *z* − 1 appear to represent consecutive integers, the problem never specifies that *z* is an integer. When you pick a fraction, $z = \dfrac{1}{2}$, you find a case that makes the statement true and also answers the question with a Yes.

(2) INSUFFICIENT: If you understand absolute value, then you might recognize that the statement $|z|$ < 1 establishes that z is between −1 and 1. If not, test some cases.

In general, start by trying the numbers that worked in the last statement. Are they valid for this statement as well? If so, this could save you time in evaluating these cases and also make it easier if and when you get to the stage of combining the two statements:

Case	z	$\|z\| < 1$	Is $z > 0$?
#1	−2	2 < 1 ✗	
#2	$\frac{1}{2}$	$\frac{1}{2} < 1$ ✓	Yes
#3	$-\frac{1}{2}$	$-\frac{1}{2} < 1$ ✓	No

For this statement, −2 is an invalid case, but $\frac{1}{2}$ is valid. That valid case returns a Yes answer, so try to find a case that will return a No answer instead. Case 3 does just that.

(1) AND (2) SUFFICIENT: Statement (2) allows any values between −1 and 1. From among these possible values, any numbers between 0 and 1 will also make statement (1) true. Therefore, z can be greater than 0.

The answer could still be (E), though, if any numbers between −1 and 0 make statement (1) true as well. Try plugging $z = -\frac{1}{2}$ into statement (1):

$$\left(-\frac{1}{2}+1\right)\left(-\frac{1}{2}\right)\left(-\frac{1}{2}-1\right) < 0?$$
$$\left(\frac{1}{2}\right)\left(-\frac{1}{2}\right)\left(-\frac{3}{2}\right) < 0?$$

Don't multiply out the left side of the equation! The two negative terms will multiply to a positive number, leaving:

positive < 0?

This, of course, is never true. It may take a little more work or reasoning to realize that this result will be repeated for any z you pick between −1 and 0. Therefore, only numbers between 0 and 1 work for both statements. The value of z has to be positive.

The correct answer is (C).

10

Chapter 11
of Algebra

Extra Equations Strategies

In This Chapter...

Simultaneous Equations: Three Equations

Complex Absolute Value Equations

Integer Constraints

Using FOIL with Square Roots

Quadratic Formula

Using Conjugates to Rationalize Denominators

Chapter 11

Extra Equations Strategies

Simultaneous Equations: Three Equations

The procedure for solving a system of three equations with three variables is exactly the same as for a system with two equations and two variables. You can use substitution or combination. This example uses both:

Solve the following for w, x, and y.

$$x + w = y$$
$$2y + w = 3x - 2$$
$$13 - 2w = x + y$$

The first equation is already solved for y:

$$y = x + w$$

Substitute for y in the second and third equations.

Substitute for y in the second equation:

$$2(x + w) + w = 3x - 2$$

$$2x + 2w + w = 3x - 2$$

$$-x + 3w = -2$$

Substitute for y in the third equation:

$$13 - 2w = x + (x + w)$$

$$13 - 2w = 2x + w$$

$$13 = 2x + 3w$$

Next, subtract one equation from the other to drop the w term.

$$2x + 3w = 13$$
$$- (-x + 3w = -2)$$
$$\overline{}$$
$$2x - (-x) = 13 - (-2)$$
$$3x = 15$$
$$x = 5$$

Therefore, $x = 5$

Use your solution for x to determine solutions for the other two variables:

$2x + 3w = 13$	$y = x + w$
$10 + 3w = 13$	$y = 5 + 1$
$3w = 3$	$y = 6$
$w = 1$	

The preceding example requires a lot of steps to solve. The GMAT is unlikely to ask you to solve for all three variables, but could ask you to solve for just one or for some other combination of variables. For more on this topic, see Chapter 7, (Strategy: Combos).

Complex Absolute Value Equations

Earlier, you learned about absolute value equations that have one unknown inside one absolute value expression. These equations can also become more complicated by including more than one absolute value expression. There are two primary types of these complex absolute value equations:

1. The equation contains *two* or more variables in more than one absolute value expression. These equations, which usually lack constants, are generally testing the concept of positives and negatives. You can learn about a more conceptual approach to positives and negatives in the *Test Cases* strategy chapter of our *Number Properties GMAT Strategy Guide*.

2. The equation contains *one* variable and at least one *constant* in more than one absolute value expression. These equations are usually easier to solve with an algebraic approach than with a conceptual approach. For example:

If $|x - 2| = |2x - 3|$, what are the possible values for x?

Because there are two absolute value expressions, each of which yields two algebraic cases, it seems that you need to test *four* cases overall: positive/positive, positive/negative, negative/positive, and negative/negative.

1. The positive/positive case: $(x - 2) = (2x - 3)$
2. The positive/negative case: $(x - 2) = -(2x - 3)$

3. The negative/positive case: $-(x-2)=(2x-3)$

4. The negative/negative case: $-(x-2)=-(2x-3)$

However, note that case (1) and case (4) yield the same equation. Likewise, case (2) and case (3) yield the same equation. Thus, you only need to consider two real cases: one in which neither expression changes sign, and another in which one expression changes sign:

CASE A: Same sign $\qquad\qquad$ CASE B: Different signs

$(x-2)=(2x-3)$ $\qquad\qquad$ $(x-2)=-(2x-3)$

$1=x$ $\qquad\qquad\qquad\qquad$ $3x=5$

$\qquad\qquad\qquad\qquad\qquad\qquad$ $x=5/3$

Complex absolute value equations have one other catch: After you finish solving the different cases, you have to check the validity of the solutions by plugging them back into the original equation. Ironically, complex absolute value equations can sometimes yield results that are not actually valid solutions.

Both solutions are valid here, because $|1-2|=|2(1)-3|=1$ and $\left|\dfrac{5}{3}-2\right|=\left|2\left(\dfrac{5}{3}\right)-3\right|=\dfrac{1}{3}$.

Integer Constraints

Occasionally, a GMAT algebra problem contains integer constraints. In such a case, there might be many possible solutions among all numbers but only one *integer* solution.

$2y-x=2xy$ and $x \neq 0$. If x and y are integers, which of the following could equal y?

(A) 2
(B) 1
(C) 0
(D) −1
(E) −2

Test the possibilities for y, using the answer choices, and find the answer that also makes x an integer. The case $y=0$ produces $x=0$, but this outcome is disallowed by the condition that $x \neq 0$. The only other case that produces an integer value for x is $y=-1$, yielding $x=2$. Thus, the answer is (**D**).

Integer constraints together with *inequalities* can also lead to just one solution.

If x and y are nonnegative integers and $x+y=25$, what is x?

(1) $20x+10y<300$
(2) $20x+10y>280$

11

First, simplify the inequality in statement (1): $2x + y < 30$. Since x and y have to be nonnegative integers, the smallest possible value for $2x + y$ is when $x = 0$ and $y = 25$: $2x + y = 25$.

If $x = 1$ and $y = 24$, then $2x + y$ is 26. Statement (1), then, yields multiple possible values for x; thus, it is not sufficient.

Simplify statement (2): $2x + y > 28$. This statement also allows multiple possible values of x. (If you're not sure, test out some numbers. If $x = 10$ and $y = 15$, then $2x + y = 35$. If $x = 15$ and $y = 10$, then $2x + y = 40$.)

Here's what happens when you combine the two statements:

Substituting $(25 - x)$ for y: $28 < 2x + y < 30$
$$28 < 2x + (25 - x) < 30$$
$$28 < x + 25 < 30$$
$$3 < x < 5$$

Since x must be an integer, x must equal 4. Therefore, the answer is **(C)**.

Using FOIL with Square Roots

Some GMAT problems ask you to solve factored expressions that involve roots. For example, the GMAT might ask you to solve the following:

What is the value of $\left(\sqrt{8} - \sqrt{3}\right)\left(\sqrt{8} + \sqrt{3}\right)$?

Even though these problems do not involve any variables, you can solve them just like you would solve a pair of quadratic factors: use FOIL:

FIRST: $\sqrt{8} \times \sqrt{8} = 8$ OUTER: $\sqrt{8} \times \sqrt{3} = \sqrt{24}$

INNER: $\sqrt{8} \times \left(-\sqrt{3}\right) = -\sqrt{24}$ LAST: $\left(\sqrt{3}\right)\left(-\sqrt{3}\right) = -3$

The four terms are: $8 + \sqrt{24} - \sqrt{24} - 3$.

You can simplify this expression by removing the two middle terms (they cancel each other out) and subtracting: $8 + \sqrt{24} - \sqrt{24} - 3 = 8 - 3 = 5$. Although the problem looks complex, using FOIL reduces the entire expression to 5.

Quadratic Formula

The vast majority of quadratic equations on the GMAT can be solved by the factoring or square-rooting techniques described earlier in this guide. However, very occasionally you might encounter a problem difficult to solve with these techniques. Such a problem requires an understanding of the quadratic formula, which can solve any quadratic equation but is cumbersome to memorize and use. Unless you are aiming to score a 51 (the top score) on the Quant section of the GMAT, you can skip this lesson.

Quadratic Formula: For any quadratic equation of the form $ax^2 + bx + c = 0$, where a, b, and c are constants, the solutions for x are given by:

$$x = \frac{-b \pm \sqrt{b^2 - 4ac}}{2a}$$

Consider the following: If $x^2 + 8x + 13 = 0$, what is x?

This problem cannot be factored because there are no two integers for which the sum is 8 and the product is 13. However, you can find the solutions by plugging the coefficients from the equation into the quadratic formula:

$$x = \frac{-8 \pm \sqrt{8^2 - 4(1)(13)}}{2(1)} = \frac{-8 \pm \sqrt{64 - 52}}{2(1)} = -4 \pm \frac{\sqrt{12}}{2} = \{-4 + \sqrt{3}, -4 - \sqrt{3}\}$$

It is not imperative that you memorize the quadratic formula, but the expression underneath the radical in the formula ($b^2 - 4ac$, called the discriminant) can convey important information: it can tell you how many solutions the equation has. If the discriminant is greater than 0, there will be two solutions. If the discriminant is equal to 0, there will be one solution. If the discriminant is less than 0, there will be no solutions. For example:

Which of the following equations has no solution for x?

    (A) $x^2 - 8x - 11 = 0$
    (B) $x^2 + 8x + 11 = 0$
    (C) $x^2 + 7x + 11 = 0$
    (D) $x^2 - 6x + 11 = 0$
    (E) $x^2 - 6x - 11 = 0$

None of these equations can be solved by factoring. However, you can determine which of the equations has no solution by determining which equation has a negative discriminant (and note that you can stop at any point that you realize the answer will not be negative):

    (A) $b^2 - 4ac = (-8)^2 - 4(1)(-11) = 64 + 44 = 108$ ⟵ For example, a positive plus a
    (B) $b^2 - 4ac = (8)^2 - 4(1)(11) = 64 - 44 = 20$ positive will be positive, so you
    (C) $b^2 - 4ac = (7)^2 - 4(1)(11) = 49 - 44 = 5$ could stop this calculation early.
    (D) $b^2 - 4ac = (-6)^2 - 4(1)(11) = 36 - 44 = -8$
    (E) $b^2 - 4ac = (-6)^2 - 4(1)(-11) = 36 + 44 = 80$

The correct answer is **(D)**. Again, it is very rare for a GMAT problem to require familiarity with the quadratic formula. The vast majority of quadratic equations can be factored through conventional methods.

11

Using Conjugates to Rationalize Denominators

Occasionally, GMAT problems involve fractions that contain square roots in the denominator. When the denominator is a square root alone, you can simplify the fraction by multiplying the numerator and denominator by the square root:

Simplify $\dfrac{4}{\sqrt{2}}$

By multiplying the numerator and denominator by the square root, you remove the root from the denominator entirely:

$$\frac{4}{\sqrt{2}} \times \left(\frac{\sqrt{2}}{\sqrt{2}} \right) = \frac{4\sqrt{2}}{2} = 2\sqrt{2}$$

However, simplifying a denominator that contains the sum or difference of a square root *and* another term is more difficult:

Simplify $\dfrac{4}{3 - \sqrt{2}}$

To simplify this type of problem, you need to use the conjugate of the denominator. The conjugate for any square root expression involving addition or subtraction is defined as follows:

For $a + \sqrt{b}$, the conjugate is given by $a - \sqrt{b}$.

For $a - \sqrt{b}$, the conjugate is given by $a + \sqrt{b}$.

In other words, change the sign of the second term to find the conjugate. By multiplying the numerator and denominator by the conjugate, you eliminate the square root from the denominator:

$$\frac{4}{3 - \sqrt{2}} \left(\frac{3 + \sqrt{2}}{3 + \sqrt{2}} \right) = \frac{4(3 + \sqrt{2})}{(3 - \sqrt{2})(3 + \sqrt{2})} = \frac{12 + 4\sqrt{2}}{9 + 3\sqrt{2} - 3\sqrt{2} - 2} = \frac{12 + 4\sqrt{2}}{7}$$

11

Problem Set

Solve each problem, applying the concepts and rules you learned in this section.

1. Given that $ab = 12$ and $\dfrac{c}{a} + 10 = 15$, what is bc?

2. If $|x + 1| = |3x - 2|$, what are the possible values for x?

    (A) $\dfrac{1}{4}$ and $\dfrac{3}{4}$

    (B) $\dfrac{1}{4}$ and $\dfrac{3}{2}$

    (C) $\dfrac{2}{3}$ and $\dfrac{3}{2}$

    (D) $\dfrac{2}{3}$ and $\dfrac{4}{3}$

    (E) $\dfrac{3}{4}$ and $\dfrac{4}{3}$

3. If $xy = 2$, $xz = 8$, and $yz = 5$, then the value of xyz is closest to:

    (A)   5
    (B)   9
    (C)   15
    (D)   25
    (E)   75

4. If $c + d = 11$ and c and d are positive integers, which of the following is a possible value for $5c + 8d$?

    (A) 55
    (B) 61
    (C) 69
    (D) 83
    (E) 88

5. If $mn = 3(m + 1) + n$ and m and n are integers, m could be any of the following values EXCEPT:

    (A) 2
    (B) 3
    (C) 4
    (D) 5
    (E) 7

11

6.   Which of the following equations has no solution for a?

(A) $a^2 - 6a + 7 = 0$
(B) $a^2 + 6a - 7 = 0$
(C) $a^2 + 4a + 3 = 0$
(D) $a^2 - 4a + 3 = 0$
(E) $a^2 - 4a + 5 = 0$

7.   Which of the following is equal to $\dfrac{6 + \sqrt{5}}{2 - \sqrt{5}}$?

(A) 17
(B) -17

(C) $17 + 8\sqrt{5}$

(D) $-17 - 8\sqrt{5}$

(E) $12 + 12\sqrt{5}$

8.   Solve for a, b, and c: $a + b = 10$, $b + c = 12$, and $a + c = 16$.

Solutions

1. **60:** You can first solve for $\dfrac{c}{a}$; then multiply the two equations together to quickly solve for bc:

$$\frac{c}{a}=15-10=5$$

$$(\cancel{a}b)\left(\frac{c}{\cancel{a}}\right)=12(5) \qquad bc=12(5)=60$$

2. **(B):** This is a complex absolute value problem, so you first must decide on an approach. The equation $|x+1|=|3x-2|$ has one variable (x) and several constants (1, 3, and −2). Thus, you should take an algebraic approach.

In theory, with two absolute value expressions, you would set up four cases. However, those four cases collapse to just two cases: 1) the two expressions inside the absolute value symbols are given the same sign, and 2) the two expressions are given the opposite sign.

Case (1): Same Sign	Case (2): Opposite Sign
$x+1=3x-2$	$x+1=-(3x-2)=-3x+2$
$3=2x$	$4x=1$
$x=\dfrac{3}{2}$	$x=\dfrac{1}{4}$

Testing each solution in the original equation, you verify that both solutions are valid:

$$\left|\frac{3}{2}+1\right|=\left|3\left(\frac{3}{2}\right)-2\right| \qquad\qquad \left|\frac{1}{4}+1\right|=\left|3\left(\frac{1}{4}\right)-2\right|$$

$$\left|\frac{5}{2}\right|=\left|\frac{9}{2}-2\right| \qquad\qquad\qquad \left|\frac{5}{4}\right|=\left|\frac{3}{4}-2\right|=\left|\frac{-5}{4}\right|$$

$$\frac{5}{2}=\frac{5}{2} \qquad\qquad\qquad\qquad\qquad \frac{5}{4}=\frac{5}{4}$$

3. **(B):** Multiplying together all three equations gives $x^2y^2z^2 = 80$. As a result, $xyz = \sqrt{80}$, which is very close to $xyz = 9$.

4. **(B):** Because c and d must be positive integers and $c + d = 11$, there are only 10 possible values for $5c + 8d$ (starting with $c = 1$ and $d = 10$, then $c = 2$ and $d = 9$, and so on). In other words, if your starting point is $5c + 8d = 58$, where $c = 10$ and $d = 1$, if you reduce c by 1 and increase d by 1, the resulting sum will increase by 3; this pattern will continue to occur all the way to your largest possible value, 85. Starting with 58, then, keep adding 3 until you reach a number found in the answers. $58 + 3 = 61$, and 61 is one of the answer choices.

11

Alternatively, you can notice that consecutive values of $5c + 8d$ differ by 3. In other words, every possible value of $5c + 8d$ equals a multiple of 3 plus some constant. By inspection, you see that the values of $5c + 8d$ are all one more than a multiple of 3: for instance, the value $82 = 81 + 1$. The only answer choice that equals a multiple of 3 plus 1 is 61: $60 + 1$.

5. **(D):** First, you need to solve for n. The reason you solve for n is that the answer choices list possible values for m, the other variable. If you solve for n, then you can plug the possible values for m into the formula and see when you get a non-integer for n, since n must be an integer:

$$mn = 3(m+1) + n$$
$$mn - n = 3(m+1)$$
$$n(m-1) = 3(m+1)$$
$$n = \frac{3(m+1)}{(m-1)} \longrightarrow$$

m	$n = \dfrac{3(m+1)}{(m-1)}$
2	$n = \dfrac{3(2+1)}{(2-1)} = 9$
3	$n = \dfrac{3(3+1)}{(3-1)} = 6$
4	$n = \dfrac{3(4+1)}{(4-1)} = 5$
5	$n = \dfrac{3(5+1)}{(5-1)} = \dfrac{18}{4} = \dfrac{9}{2}$
7	$n = \dfrac{3(7+1)}{(7-1)} = 4$

Only a value of 5 for m does not produce an integer for n.

6. **(E):** You can determine which of the equations has no solution by determining which equation has a negative discriminant:

(A) $b^2 - 4ac = (-6)^2 - 4(1)(7) = 36 - 28 = 8$
(B) $b^2 - 4ac = (6)^2 - 4(1)(-7) = 36 + 28 = 64$
(C) $b^2 - 4ac = (4)^2 - 4(1)(3) = 16 - 12 = 4$
(D) $b^2 - 4ac = (-4)^2 - 4(1)(3) = 16 - 12 = 4$
(E) $b^2 - 4ac = (-4)^2 - 4(1)(5) = 16 - 20 = -4$

7. **(D):** In order to simplify a fraction that has a difference involving a square root in the denominator, you need to multiply the numerator and denominator by the sum of the same terms (this is also known as the "conjugate"):

$$\frac{6+\sqrt{5}}{2-\sqrt{5}} = \frac{6+\sqrt{5}}{2-\sqrt{5}} \times \frac{2+\sqrt{5}}{2+\sqrt{5}} = \frac{(6+\sqrt{5})(2+\sqrt{5})}{2^2 - (\sqrt{5})^2} = \frac{12 + 2\sqrt{5} + 6\sqrt{5} + 5}{4-5} = \frac{17 + 8\sqrt{5}}{-1} = -17 - 8\sqrt{5}$$

8. $a = 7$; $b = 3$; $c = 9$: This problem could be solved by an elaborate series of substitutions. However, because the coefficients on each variable in each equation are equal to 1, combination proves easier. Here is one way, though certainly not the only way, to solve the problem:

First, combine all three equations by adding them together. Then divide by 2 to get the sum of all three equations. Subtracting any of the original equations from this new equation will solve for one of the variables, and the rest can be solved by plugging back into the original equations.

$$
\begin{array}{rl}
a + b & = 10 \\
b + c & = 12 \\
a + c & = 16 \\
\hline
2a + 2b + 2c & = 38
\end{array}
$$

$$
\begin{array}{rl}
a + b + c & = 19 \\
-(a + b & = 10) \\
\hline
c & = 9
\end{array}
$$

$$
\begin{array}{l}
b + 9 = 12 \\
b = 3
\end{array}
\qquad
\begin{array}{l}
a + 9 = 16 \\
a = 7
\end{array}
$$

11

Chapter 12
of
Algebra

Extra Formulas Strategies

In This Chapter...

Chapter 12

Extra Formulas Strategies

Sequences and Patterns

Some sequences are easier to look at in terms of patterns, rather than rules. For example, consider the following:

> If $S_n = 3^n$, what is the units digit of S_{65}?

Clearly, you cannot be expected to multiply out 3^{65} on the GMAT. Therefore, there must be a pattern in the units digits of the powers of three:

$3^1 = \mathbf{3}$
$3^2 = \mathbf{9}$
$3^3 = 2\mathbf{7}$
$3^4 = 8\mathbf{1}$
$3^5 = 24\mathbf{3}$
$3^6 = 72\mathbf{9}$
$3^7 = 2,18\mathbf{7}$
$3^8 = 6,56\mathbf{1}$

Note the pattern of the units digits in the powers of 3: 3, 9, 7, 1, [repeating]…. Also note that the units digit of S_n, when n is a multiple of 4, is always equal to 1. You can use the multiples of 4 as "anchor points" in the pattern. Since 65 is 1 more than 64 (the closest multiple of 4), the units digit of S_{65} will be 3, which always follows 1 in the pattern.

As a side note, most sequences on the GMAT are defined for integer $n \geq 1$. That is, the sequence S_n almost always starts at S_1. Occasionally, a sequence might start at S_0, but in that case, you are told that $n \geq 0$. Notice that the *first* term in the sequence would then be S_0, the *second* term would be S_1, the *third* term would be S_2, and so on.

Compound Functions

Compound functions give you two different rules to use.

If $f(x) = x^3 + \sqrt{x}$ and $g(x) = 4x - 3$, what is $f(g(3))$?

The expression $f(g(3))$, pronounced "f of g of 3", looks ugly, but the key to solving compound function problems is to work from the *inside out*. In this case, start with $g(3)$. Start by putting the number 3 into the function $g(x)$:

$$g(3) = 4(3) - 3 = 12 - 3 = 9$$

Use the result from the *inner* function g as the new input variable for the *outer* function f:

$$f(g(3)) = f(9) = (9)^3 + \sqrt{9} = 729 + 3 = 732 \qquad \text{The final result is 732.}$$

Note that changing the order of the compound functions changes the answer:

If $f(x) = x^3 + \sqrt{x}$ and $g(x) = 4x - 3$, what is $g(f(3))$?

Again, work from the inside out. This time, start with $f(3)$ (which is now the inner function):

$$f(3) = (3)^3 + \sqrt{3} = 27 + \sqrt{3}$$

Use the result from the *inner* function, f, as the new input variable for the *outer* function g:

$$g(f(3)) = g(27 + \sqrt{3}) = 4(27 + \sqrt{3}) - 3 = 108 + 4\sqrt{3} - 3 = 105 + 4\sqrt{3}$$

Thus, $g(f(3)) = 105 + 4\sqrt{3}$.

In general, $f(g(x))$ and $g(f(x))$ are not the same rule overall and will often lead to different outcomes. As an analogy, think of "putting on socks" and "putting on shoes" as two functions: the order in which you perform these steps obviously matters!

You may be asked to *find* a value of x for which $f(g(x)) = g(f(x))$. In that case, use *variable substitution*, working as always from the inside out:

If $f(x) = x^2 + 1$, and $g(x) = 2x$, for what positive value of x does $f(g(x)) = g(f(x))$?

Evaluate as shown in the problems above, using x instead of an actual value:

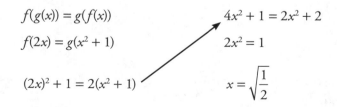

$$f(g(x)) = g(f(x)) \qquad\qquad 4x^2 + 1 = 2x^2 + 2$$
$$f(2x) = g(x^2 + 1) \qquad\qquad 2x^2 = 1$$
$$(2x)^2 + 1 = 2(x^2 + 1) \qquad\qquad x = \sqrt{\frac{1}{2}}$$

Take only the positive root since x must be positive.

MANHATTAN
PREP

Functions with Unknown Constants

On the GMAT, you may be given a function with an unknown constant. You will also be given the value of the function for a specific number. You can combine these pieces of information to find the complete function rule:

> If $f(x) = ax^2 - x$, and $f(4) = 28$, what is $f(-2)$?

Solve these problems in three steps. First, use the value of the input variable and the corresponding output value of the function to solve for the unknown constant:

$$f(4) = a(4)^2 - 4 = 28$$
$$16a - 4 = 28$$
$$16a = 32$$
$$a = 2$$

Then, rewrite the function, replacing the constant with its numerical value:

$$f(x) = ax^2 - x = 2x^2 - x$$

Finally, solve the function for the new input variable:

$$f(-2) = 2(-2)^2 - (-2) = 8 + 2 = 10$$

Function Graphs

A function can be visualized by graphing it in the coordinate plane. The input variable is considered the domain of the function, or the x-coordinate. The corresponding output is considered the range of the function, or the y-coordinate. This is rarely tested on the GMAT; unless you are aiming for the top Quant score of 51, you can skip this lesson. Consider the following:

> What is the graph of the function $f(x) = -2x^2 + 1$?

Create an INPUT–OUTPUT table by evaluating the function for several input values. Then, plot points to see the shape of the graph:

INPUT	OUTPUT	(x, y)
-1	$-2(-1)^2 + 1 = -1$	$(-1, -1)$
0	$-2(0)^2 + 1 = 1$	$(0, 1)$
1	$-2(1)^2 + 1 = -1$	$(1, -1)$

12

It may be sufficient to calculate only 3 or 4 values as long as you have found the pattern and can accurately represent the graph. For more on graphing in general, see the *Coordinate Plane* chapter of Manhattan Prep's *Geometry GMAT Strategy Guide*.

Common Function Types

Though the GMAT could pose function questions in many different forms, several different themes occur through many of them. This section explores some of these common types of functions.

Population Problems

In these problems, some population typically increases by a common factor every time period. These can be solved with a population chart. Consider the following example:

> The population of a certain type of bacterium triples every 10 minutes. If the population of a colony 20 minutes ago was 100, in approximately how many minutes from now will the bacteria population reach 24,000?

Make a table with a few rows, labeling one of the middle rows as NOW. Work forward, backward, or both (as necessary in the problem), obeying any conditions given in the problem statement about the rate of growth or decay. In this case, triple each population number as you move down a row. Notice that while the population increases by a constant *factor*, it does *not* increase by a constant *amount* each time period.

For this problem, the population chart at right shows that the bacterial population will reach 24,000 about 30 minutes from now.

In some cases, you might pick a *smart number* for a starting point in your population chart. If you do so, pick a number that makes the computations as easy as possible.

Time Elapsed	Population
20 minutes ago	100
10 minutes ago	300
NOW	900
in 10 minutes	2,700
in 20 minutes	8,100
in 30 minutes	24,300

Proportionality

Many GMAT problems, especially those concerned with real-life situations, will use direct or inverse proportionality between the input and the output values.

Direct proportionality means that the two quantities always change by the same factor and in the same direction. For instance, tripling the input will cause the output to triple as well. Cutting the input in half will also cut the output in half. Direct proportionality relationships are of the form $y = kx$, where x is the input value, y is the output value, and k is called the proportionality constant. This equation can also be written as $\frac{y}{x} = k$, which means that the ratio of the output and input values is always constant.

12

The maximum height reached by an object thrown directly upward is directly proportional to the square of the velocity with which the object is thrown. If an object thrown upward at 16 feet per second reaches a maximum height of 4 feet, with what speed must the object be thrown upward to reach a maximum height of 9 feet?

Typically, with direct proportion problems, you will be given *before* and *after* values. Set up ratios to solve the problem. For example, $\dfrac{y_1}{x_1}$ can be used for the *before* values and $\dfrac{y_2}{x_2}$ can be used for the *after* values. Write $\dfrac{y_1}{x_1} = \dfrac{y_2}{x_2}$, since both ratios are equal to the same constant k. Finally, solve for the unknowns.

In the problem given above, be sure to note that the direct proportion is between the height and the square of the velocity, not the velocity itself. Therefore, write the proportion as $\dfrac{h_1}{v_1^{\,2}} = \dfrac{h_2}{v_2^{\,2}}$. Substitute the known values $h_1 = 4$, $v_1 = 16$, and $h_2 = 9$:

$$\frac{4}{16^2} = \frac{9}{v_2^{\,2}} \qquad v_2^{\,2} = 9\left(\frac{16^2}{4}\right) \qquad v_2^{\,2} = 9(64) = 576 \qquad v_2 = 24$$

Thus, the object must be thrown upward at 24 feet per second.

Inverse proportionality means that the two quantities change by *reciprocal* factors. Cutting the input in half will actually double the output. Tripling the input will cut the output to one-third of its original value.

Inverse proportionality relationships are of the form $y = \dfrac{k}{x}$, where x is the input value, y is the output value, and k is the proportionality constant. This equation can also be written as $yx = k$, which means that the product of the output and input values is always constant.

As with other proportion problems, you will typically be given *before* and *after* values. However, this time you set up products, not ratios, to solve the problem—for example, y_1x_1 can be used for the *before* values and y_2x_2 can be used for the *after* values. Next, write $y_1x_1 = y_2x_2$, since each product equals the same constant k. Finally, use algebra to solve for the unknowns in the problem. Try this example:

The amount of electrical current that flows through a wire is inversely proportional to the resistance in that wire. If a wire currently carries 4 amperes of electrical current, but the resistance is then cut to one-third of its original value, how many amperes of electrical current will flow through the wire?

While you are not given precise amounts for the *before* or *after* resistance in the wire, you can pick numbers. Using 3 as the original resistance and 1 as the new resistance, the new electrical current will be 12 amperes:

$$C_1R_1 = C_2R_2 \qquad 4(3) = C_2(1) \qquad 12 = C_2$$

12

Linear Growth

Many GMAT problems, especially word problems, feature quantities with linear growth (or decay), that is, they grow (or decline) at a constant rate. Such quantities are determined by the linear function: $y = mx + b$. In this equation, the slope m is the constant rate at which the quantity grows. The y-intercept b is the value of the quantity at time zero, and the variable (in this case, x) stands for time. You can also use t to represent time.

For instance, if a baby weighs 9 pounds at birth and gains 1.2 pounds per month, then the baby's weight can be written as $W = 1.2t + 9$, where t is the baby's age in months. Note that $t = 0$ represents the birth of the baby.

> Jake was 4½ feet tall on his 12th birthday, when he began to have a growth spurt. Between his 12th and 15th birthdays, he grew at a constant rate. If Jake was 20% taller on his 15th birthday than on his 13th birthday, how many inches per year did Jake grow during his growth spurt? (12 inches = 1 foot)

In this problem, the constant growth does not begin until Jake has reached his 12th birthday, so in order to use the constant growth function $y = mx + b$, let time $x = 0$ (the initial state) stand for Jake's 12th birthday. Therefore, $x = 1$ stands for his 13th birthday, $x = 2$ stands for his 14th birthday, and $x = 3$ stands for his 15th birthday.

The problem asks for an answer in inches but gives you information in feet. Therefore, convert to inches at the beginning of the problem: 4½ feet = 54 inches = b. Since the growth rate m is unknown, the growth function can be written as $y = mx + 54$. Jake's height on his 13th birthday, when $x = 1$, was $54 + m$, and his height on his 15th birthday, when $x = 3$, was $54 + 3m$. Because the problem also states that Jake was 20% taller on his 15th birthday than on his 13th, you can write an equation:

$$54 + 3m = (54 + m) + 0.20(54 + m) \qquad 1.8m = 10.8$$
$$54 + 3m = 1.2(54 + m) \qquad\qquad\qquad m = 6$$
$$54 + 3m = 64.8 + 1.2m$$

Therefore, Jake grew at a rate of 6 inches each year.

Symmetry

Some difficult GMAT function questions revolve around symmetry, or the property that two seemingly different inputs to the function always yield the same output.

12

For which of the following functions does $f(x) = f\left(\dfrac{1}{x}\right)$, given that $x \neq -2, -1, 0,$ or 1?

(A) $f(x) = \left|\dfrac{x+1}{x}\right|$ (B) $f(x) = \left|\dfrac{x+1}{x-1}\right|$ (C) $f(x) = \left|\dfrac{x-1}{x}\right|$

(D) $f(x) = \left|\dfrac{x}{x+1}\right|$ (E) $f(x) = \left|\dfrac{x+1}{x+2}\right|$

There are two primary ways that you can set about solving this problem. First, you could substitute $\dfrac{1}{x}$ in for x in each of the functions and simplify, to see which of the functions yields the same result. Alternatively, you could pick a number for x and see which of the functions produces an equal output for both x and $\dfrac{1}{x}$. In most cases, the latter strategy will probably be easier. For example, you could choose $x = 3$:

		$f(3)$	$f\left(\dfrac{1}{3}\right)$
(A)	$f(x) = \left|\dfrac{x+1}{x}\right|$	$\left|\dfrac{3+1}{3}\right| = \dfrac{4}{3}$	$\left|\dfrac{\frac{1}{3}+1}{\frac{1}{3}}\right| = \left|\dfrac{\frac{4}{3}}{\frac{1}{3}}\right| = 4$
(B)	$f(x) = \left|\dfrac{x+1}{x-1}\right|$	$\left|\dfrac{3+1}{3-1}\right| = \dfrac{4}{2} = 2$	$\left|\dfrac{\frac{1}{3}+1}{\frac{1}{3}-1}\right| = \left|\dfrac{\frac{4}{3}}{-\frac{2}{3}}\right| = 2$
(C)	$f(x) = \left|\dfrac{x-1}{x}\right|$	$\left|\dfrac{3-1}{3}\right| = \dfrac{2}{3}$	$\left|\dfrac{\frac{1}{3}-1}{\frac{1}{3}}\right| = \left|\dfrac{-\frac{2}{3}}{\frac{1}{3}}\right| = 2$
(D)	$f(x) = \left|\dfrac{x}{x+1}\right|$	$\left|\dfrac{3}{3+1}\right| = \dfrac{3}{4}$	$\left|\dfrac{\frac{1}{3}}{\frac{1}{3}+1}\right| = \left|\dfrac{\frac{1}{3}}{\frac{4}{3}}\right| = \dfrac{1}{4}$
(E)	$f(x) = \left|\dfrac{x+1}{x+2}\right|$	$\left|\dfrac{3+1}{3+2}\right| = \dfrac{4}{5}$	$\left|\dfrac{\frac{1}{3}+1}{\frac{1}{3}+2}\right| = \left|\dfrac{\frac{4}{3}}{\frac{7}{3}}\right| = \dfrac{4}{7}$

12

Only answer **(B)** returns the same result for 3 and $\frac{1}{3}$, so it is the correct answer. Note that, if you are confident with your math, you can stop after testing (B) and finding that it does work. You can also prove that (B) is the correct answer algebraically:

$$f(x) = \left| \frac{x+1}{x-1} \right|$$

$$f\left(\frac{1}{x}\right) = \left| \frac{\frac{1}{x}+1}{\frac{1}{x}-1} \right| = \left| \frac{\frac{x+1}{x}}{\frac{1-x}{x}} \right| = \left| \frac{x+1}{1-x} \right| = \left| \frac{x+1}{-(1-x)} \right| = \left| \frac{x+1}{x-1} \right|$$

In the second to last step, $-(1-x)$ replaces $1-x$ from the previous step. Technically, one of these expressions is positive and the other is negative; because they are inside of an absolute value symbol, however, they both become positive.

Problem Set

1. If $g(x) = \dfrac{x^3 - ax}{4}$, and $g(2) = \dfrac{1}{2}$, what is the value of $g(4)$?

2. The velocity of a falling object in a vacuum is directly proportional to the amount of time the object has been falling. If after 5 seconds an object is falling at a speed of 90 miles per hour, how fast will it be falling after 12 seconds?

3. If $S_n = (4^n) + 3$, what is the units digit of S_{100}?

4. The "luminous flux," or perceived brightness, of a light source is measured in lumens and is inversely proportional to the square of the distance from the light. If a light source produces 200 lumens at a distance of 3 meters, at what distance will the light source produce a luminous flux of 25 lumens?

5. For which of the following functions does $f(x) = f(2 - x)$?

   (A) $f(x) = x + 2$
   (B) $f(x) = 2x - x^2$
   (C) $f(x) = 2 - x$
   (D) $f(x) = (2 - x)^2$
   (E) $f(x) = x^2$

6. If $f(x) = (x + \sqrt{3})^4$, what is the range of the function $f(x)$?

   (A) $\sqrt{3} < f(x) < 4$
   (B) $f(x) \geq 0$
   (C) $f(x) < 0$
   (D) $f(x) \neq 0$

7. If $g(x) = 3x + \sqrt{x}$, what is the value of $g(d^2 + 6d + 9)$?

12

Solutions

1. **13:** $g(2) = \dfrac{(2)^3 - a(2)}{4} = \dfrac{1}{2}$

$8 - 2a = 2$

$2a = 6 \qquad \rightarrow \qquad g(x) = \dfrac{x^3 - 3x}{4} \qquad \rightarrow \qquad g(4) = \dfrac{(4)^3 - 3(4)}{4} = \dfrac{\cancel{4}(4^2 - 3(1))}{\cancel{4}} = \dfrac{16 - 3}{1} = 13$

$a = 3$

2. **216 miles per hour:** Because the velocity and the time spent falling are directly proportional, you can simply set the ratio of the "before" velocity and time to the "after" velocity and time:

$$\frac{v_1}{w_1} = \frac{v_2}{w_2}$$

$$\frac{90 \text{ mph}}{5 \text{ sec}} = \frac{v_2}{12 \text{ sec}}$$

$$v_2 = \frac{90(12)}{5} = 216 \text{ mph}$$

3. **9:** Begin by listing the first few terms of the sequence in order to find the pattern:

$$S_1 = 4^1 + 3 = 4 + 3 = 7$$
$$S_2 = 4^2 + 3 = 16 + 3 = 19$$
$$S_3 = 4^3 + 3 = 64 + 3 = 67$$
$$S_4 = 4^4 + 3 = 256 + 3 = 259$$

The units digit of all odd-numbered terms is 7. The units digit of all even-numbered terms is 9. Because S_{100} is an even-numbered term, its units digit will be 9.

4. **$6\sqrt{2}$ meters (or $\sqrt{72}$ meters):** Because the intensity of the light source and the *square* of the distance are inversely proportional, you can write the product of the "before" intensity and distance squared and the product of the "after" intensity and distance squared. Then set these two products equal to each other:

$$I_1 \times d_1^{\,2} = I_2 \times d_2^{\,2}$$
$$(200 \text{ lumens})(3 \text{ meters})^2 = (25 \text{ lumens}) \times d_2^{\,2}$$
$$d_2^{\,2} = \frac{(200 \text{ lumens})(3 \text{ meters})^2}{(25 \text{ lumens})}$$
$$d_2 = 6\sqrt{2} \text{ meters}$$

12

5. **(B):** This is a "symmetry function" type of problem. Generally the easiest way to solve these kinds of problems is to pick numbers and plug them into each function to determine which answer gives the desired result. For example, you could pick $x = 4$:

		$f(4)$	$f(2-4)$ or $f(-2)$
(A)	$f(x) = x + 2$	$4 + 2 = 6$	$-2 + 2 = 0$
(B)	$f(x) = 2x - x^2$	$2(4) - 4^2 = -8$	$2(-2) - (-2)^2 = -8$
(C)	$f(x) = 2 - x$	$2 - 4 = -2$	$2 - (-2) = 4$
(D)	$f(x) = (2 - x)^2$	$(2 - 4)^2 = 4$	$[2 - (-2)]^2 = 4^2 = 16$
(E)	$f(x) = x^2$	$4^2 = 16$	$(-2)^2 = 4$

6. **(B):** If $f(x) = (x + \sqrt{3})^4$, the range of outputs, or y-values, can never be negative. Regardless of the value of x, raising $x + \sqrt{3}$ to an even power will result in a non-negative y-value. Therefore, the range of the function is all non-negative numbers, or $f(x) \geq 0$.

7. $3d^2 + 19d + 30$ **OR** $3d^2 + 17d + 24$:

$$g(d^2 + 6d + 9) = 3(d^2 + 6d + 9) + \sqrt{d^2 + 6d + 9}$$
$$= 3d^2 + 18d + 27 + \sqrt{(d + 3)^2}$$
$$= 3d^2 + 18d + 27 + d + 3 \qquad \text{OR} \qquad 3d^2 + 18d + 27 - (d + 3)$$
$$= 3d^2 + 19d + 30 \qquad\qquad \text{OR} \qquad 3d^2 + 17d + 24$$
$$\text{(if } d + 3 > 0\text{)} \qquad\qquad\qquad \text{(if } d + 3 < 0\text{)}$$

Chapter 13

of

13

Algebra

Extra Inequalities Strategies

In This Chapter...

Extra Inequalities Strategies

Optimization Problems

Optimization problems involve minimizing or maximizing values. In these problems, you need to focus on the largest and smallest possible values for each of the variables, as some combination of them will usually lead to the largest or smallest possible result.

> If $2y + 3 \leq 11$ and $1 \leq x \leq 5$, what is the maximum possible value for xy?

Test the extreme values for x and for y to determine which combinations of extreme values will maximize xy:

$$2y + 3 \leq 11 \qquad 2y \leq 8 \qquad y \leq 4$$

Extreme Values for x	**Extreme Values for y**
The lowest value for x is 1.	There is no lower limit to y.
The highest value for x is 5.	The highest value for y is 4.

Now consider the different extreme value scenarios for x, y, and xy. Since y has no lower limit and x is positive, the product xy has no lower limit. Using y's highest value (4), test the extreme values of x (1 and 5). The first extreme value generates $xy = (1)(4) = 4$. The second extreme value generates $xy = (5)(4) = 20$.

In this case, xy is maximized when $x = 5$ and $y = 4$, with a result that $xy = 20$.

> If $-7 \leq a \leq 6$ and $-7 \leq b \leq 8$, what is the maximum possible value for ab?

Once again, you are looking for a maximum possible value, this time for *ab*. Test the extreme values for *a* and for *b* to determine which combinations of extreme values will maximize *ab*:

Extreme Values for *a*	**Extreme Values for *b***
The lowest value for *a* is −7.	The lowest value for *b* is −7.
The highest value for *a* is 6.	The highest value for *b* is 8.

Now consider the different extreme value scenarios for *a*, *b*, and *ab*:

a		*b*		*ab*
Min	−7	Min	−7	$(-7) \times (-7) = \mathbf{49}$
Min	−7	Max	8	$(-7) \times 8 = -56$
Max	6	Min	−7	$6 \times (-7) = -42$
Max	6	Max	8	$6 \times 8 = 48$

This time, *ab* is maximized when you take the *negative* extreme values for both *a* and *b*, resulting in *ab* = 49. Notice that you could have focused right away on the first and fourth scenarios, because they are the only scenarios that produce positive products.

Inequalities and Absolute Value

Absolute value can be a confusing concept—particularly in a problem involving inequalities. For these types of problems, it is often helpful to try to visualize the problem with a number line.

For an equation such as $|x| = 5$, the graph of the solutions looks like this:

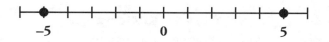

When absolute value is used in an inequality, the unknown generally has more than two possible solutions. Indeed, for an inequality such as $|x| < 5$, the graph of the solutions covers a range:

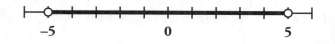

One way to understand this inequality is to say "*x* must be less than 5 units from 0 on the number line." Indeed, one interpretation of absolute value is simply distance on the number line. For a simple absolute value expression such as $|x|$, you are evaluating distance from 0.

Absolute values can be more difficult to graph than the one above. Consider, for instance, the inequality $|x + 2| < 5$. The "+ 2" term complicates things.

MANHATTAN
PREP

13

However, there is a relatively straightforward way to think about this problem. First, create a number line for the term inside the absolute value bars:

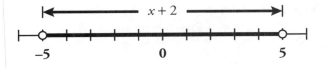

In other words, $x + 2$ must be less than 5 units away from 0 on the number line. Next, how does the "+ 2" change the graph? It shifts the entire graph down by 2, because the absolute value expression will be equal to 0 when $x = -2$. Thus, the graph for x alone will look like this:

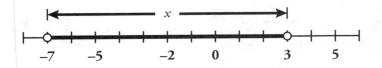

Notice that the center point for the possible values of x is now -2, which is the value for x that fits $x + 2 = 0$. This is the *center point* for the number line graph. The distance from the center point (-2) to either end point remains the same.

From this example, you can extract a standard formula for interpreting absolute value. When $|x + b| = c$, the center point of the graph is $-b$. The equation indicates that x must be *exactly* c units away from $-b$. Similarly, for the inequality $|x + b| < c$, the center point of the graph is $-b$, and x must be *less than* c units away from $-b$.

> **What is the graph of $|x - 4| < 3$?**

Based on this formula, the center point of the graph is $-(-4) = 4$, and x must be less than 3 units away from that point:

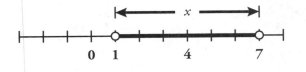

You can also solve these types of problems algebraically. Recall that equations involving absolute value require you to consider *two* scenarios: one where the expression inside the absolute value brackets is positive and one where the expression is negative. The same is true for inequalities. For example:

> **Given that $|x - 2| < 5$, what is the range of possible values for x?**

To work out the positive scenario, remove the absolute value brackets and solve:

$$|x - 2| < 5 \qquad\qquad x - 2 < 5 \qquad\qquad x < 7$$

To work out the negative scenario, reverse the signs of the terms inside the absolute value brackets, remove the brackets, and solve again:

$$|x - 2| < 5$$
$$-(x - 2) < 5$$
$$-x + 2 < 5$$
$$-x < 3$$
$$x > -3$$

Combine these two scenarios into one range of values for x: $-3 < x < 7$. This range is illustrated by the following number line:

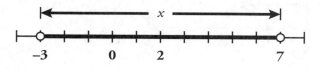

Note that this range fits in perfectly with the number-line interpretation of absolute value: this graph is the set of all points such that x is less than 5 units away from $-(-2) = 2$.

As an aside, *never* change $|x - 5|$ to $x + 5$. This is a common mistake. Remember, when you drop the absolute value signs, you either leave the expression alone or enclose the *entire* expression in parentheses and put a negative sign in front.

Reciprocals of Inequalities

Taking reciprocals of inequalities is similar to multiplying or dividing by negative numbers. You need to consider the positive and negative cases of the variables involved. The general rule is that **if $x < y$, then:**

- $\dfrac{1}{x} > \dfrac{1}{y}$ **when x and y are positive.** Flip the inequality. If $3 < 5$, then $\dfrac{1}{3} > \dfrac{1}{5}$.

- $\dfrac{1}{x} > \dfrac{1}{y}$ **when x and y are negative.** Flip the inequality. If $-4 < -2$, then $\dfrac{1}{-4} > \dfrac{1}{-2}$.

- $\dfrac{1}{x} < \dfrac{1}{y}$ **when x is negative and y is positive.** Do *not* flip the inequality.

    If $-6 < 7$, then $\dfrac{1}{-6} < \dfrac{1}{7}$. The left side is negative, while the right side is positive.

If you do not know the sign of x or y, you cannot take reciprocals.

In summary, if you know the signs of the variables, flip the inequality *unless* x and y have different signs.

13

MANHATTAN
PREP

Given that $ab < 0$ and $a > b$, which of the following must be true?

I. $a > 0$
II. $b > 0$
III. $\dfrac{1}{a} > \dfrac{1}{b}$

(A) I only
(B) II only
(C) I and III only
(D) II and III only
(E) I, II and III

If $ab < 0$, then a and b have different signs. Since $a > b$, a must be positive and b must be negative. Therefore, statement I is true, while statement II is not true.

You also know from the discussion on reciprocals that if $a > b$, then $\dfrac{1}{a} > \dfrac{1}{b}$ when a and b have different signs.

Therefore, statement III is also true and the correct answer is **(C)**.

Squaring Inequalities

As with reciprocals, you cannot square both sides of an inequality unless you know the signs of both sides of the inequality. However, the rules for squaring inequalities are somewhat different than those for reciprocating inequalities:

- **If both sides are known to be negative, then flip the inequality sign when you square.** For instance, if $x < -3$, then the left side must be negative. Since both sides are negative, you can square both sides and reverse the inequality sign: $x^2 > 9$. However, if you are given an inequality such as $x > -3$, then you cannot square both sides, because it is unclear whether the left side is positive or negative. If x is negative, then $x^2 < 9$, but if x is positive, then x^2 could be either greater than 9 or less than 9.

- **If both sides are known to be positive, then do not flip the inequality sign when you square.** For instance, if $x > 3$, then the left side must be positive; since both sides are positive, you can square both sides to yield $x^2 > 9$. If you are given an inequality such as $x < 3$, however, then you cannot square both sides, because it is unclear whether the left side is positive or negative. If x is positive, then $x^2 < 9$, but if x is negative, then x^2 could be either greater than 9 or less than 9.

- **If one side is positive and one side is negative, then you cannot square.** If you know that $x < y$, x is negative, and y is positive, you cannot make any determination about x^2 vs. y^2. If, for example, $x = -2$ and $y = 2$, then $x^2 = y^2$. If $x = -2$ and $y = 3$, then $x^2 < y^2$. If $x = -2$ and $y = 1$,

MANHATTAN
PREP

then $x^2 > y^2$. If one side of the inequality is negative and the other side is positive, then squaring is probably not warranted—some other technique is likely needed to solve the problem.

- **If the signs are unclear, then you cannot square.** Put simply, you would not know whether to flip the sign of the inequality once you have squared it.

Is $x^2 > y^2$?

   (1) $x > y$
   (2) $x > 0$

In this problem, statement (1) is insufficient, because you do not know whether x and y are positive or negative numbers. For example, if $x = 5$ and $y = 4$, then $x^2 > y^2$. However, if $x = -4$ and $y = -5$, then $x > y$ but $x^2 < y^2$.

Statement (2) does not tell you anything about y, so it too is insufficient.

Combined, you know that x is positive and larger than y. This is still insufficient, because y could be a negative number of larger magnitude than x. For example, if $x = 3$ and $y = 2$, then $x^2 > y^2$, but if $x = 3$ and $y = -4$, then $x^2 < y^2$. Therefore, the correct answer is (**E**).

Problem Set

1. If a and b are integers and $-4 \leq a \leq 3$ and $-4 \leq b \leq 5$, what is the maximum possible value for ab?

2. Is $mn > -12$?

    (1) $m > -3$
    (2) $n > -4$

3. If $\dfrac{4}{x} < \dfrac{1}{3}$, what is the possible range of values for x?

4. If $\dfrac{4}{x} < -\dfrac{1}{3}$, what is the possible range of values for x?

5. Is $x < y$?

    (1) $\dfrac{1}{x} < \dfrac{1}{y}$

    (2) $\dfrac{x}{y} < 0$

Solutions

1. **16:** In order to maximize ab, you need to test the endpoints of the ranges for a and b:

> If $a = -4$ and $b = -4$, $ab = 16$.
> If $a = -4$ and $b = 5$, the product is negative (smaller than 16).
> If $a = 3$ and $b = -4$, the product is negative (smaller than 16).
> If $a = 3$ and $b = 5$, $ab = 15$.

Thus, the maximum value for ab is 16. Notice that this maximum occurs when a and b are both negative in this case.

2. **(E):** Combining the two statements, it is tempting to conclude that mn must either be positive or a negative number larger than -12. However, because either variable could be positive or negative, it is possible to end up with a negative number less than -12. For example, m could equal -1 and n could equal 50. In that case, $mn = -50$, which is less than -12. Therefore, the two statements combined are INSUFFICIENT. The correct answer is (E).

3. **$x < 0$ OR $x > 12$:** For this type of problem, you have to consider two possibilities: x could be positive or negative. When you multiply the inequality by x, you will need to flip the sign when x is negative, but not flip the sign when x is positive:

Case 1: $x > 0$	**Case 2: $x < 0$**
$\dfrac{4}{x} < \dfrac{1}{3}$	$\dfrac{4}{x} < \dfrac{1}{3}$
$12 < x$	$12 > x$ (flip the sign because x is negative)

For Case 1, x must be positive AND greater than 12. Thus, $x > 12$.

For Case 2, x must be negative AND less than 12. Thus, $x < 0$.

Combined, $x < 0$ OR $x > 12$.

4. **$-12 < x < 0$:** For this type of problem, you have to consider two possibilities: x could be positive or negative. When you multiply the inequality by x, you will need to flip the sign when x is negative, but not flip the sign when x is positive. However, notice that x *cannot* be positive: the left-hand side of the inequality is less than $-\dfrac{1}{3}$, which means $\dfrac{4}{x}$ must be negative. Therefore, x must be negative:

Case 1: $x > 0$	Case 2: $x < 0$
Not Possible	$\dfrac{4}{x} < -\dfrac{1}{3}$ $12 > -x$ (flip the sign because x is negative) $-12 < x$ (divide by -1, flip it again)

Case 1 is not possible.

For Case 2, x must be negative AND greater than -12. Thus, $-12 < x < 0$.

5. **(C):** (1) INSUFFICIENT: The meaning of statement (1) depends on the signs of x and y. If x and y are either both positive or both negative, then you can take reciprocals of both sides, yielding $x > y$. However, this statement could also be true if x is negative and y is positive; in that case, $x < y$.

(2) INSUFFICIENT: Statement (2) tells you that the quotient of x and y is negative. In that case, x and y have different signs: one is positive and the other is negative. However, this does not tell you which one is positive and which one is negative.

(1) AND (2) SUFFICIENT: Combining the two statements, if you know that the reciprocal of x is less than that of y, and that x and y have opposite signs, then x must be negative and y must be positive, so $x < y$.

The correct answer is **(C)**.

Appendix A

of

Algebra

Data Sufficiency

In This Chapter...

Appendix A
Data Sufficiency

Data Sufficiency (DS) problems are a cross between math and logic. Imagine that your boss just walked into your office and dumped a bunch of papers on your desk, saying, "Hey, our client wants to know whether they should raise the price on this product. Can you answer that question from this data? If so, which pieces do we need to prove the case?" What would you do?

The client has asked a specific question: should the company raise the price? You have to decide which pieces of information will allow you to answer that question—or, possibly, that you don't have enough information to answer the question at all.

This kind of logical reasoning is exactly what you use when you answer DS questions.

How Data Sufficiency Works

If you already feel comfortable with the basics of Data Sufficiency, you may want to move quickly through this particular section of the chapter—but you are encouraged to read it. There are a few insights that you may find useful.

Every DS problem has the same basic form:

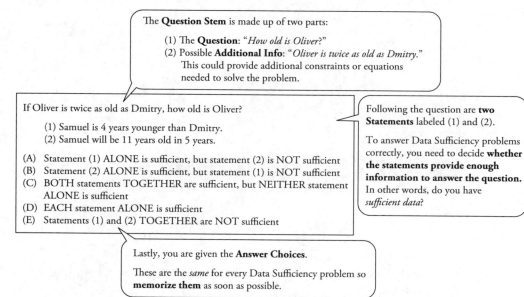

The **Question Stem** is made up of two parts:

(1) The **Question**: "*How old is Oliver?*"
(2) Possible **Additional Info**: "*Oliver is twice as old as Dmitry.*"
    This could provide additional constraints or equations
    needed to solve the problem.

If Oliver is twice as old as Dmitry, how old is Oliver?

(1) Samuel is 4 years younger than Dmitry.
(2) Samuel will be 11 years old in 5 years.

(A) Statement (1) ALONE is sufficient, but statement (2) is NOT sufficient
(B) Statement (2) ALONE is sufficient, but statement (1) is NOT sufficient
(C) BOTH statements TOGETHER are sufficient, but NEITHER statement
     ALONE is sufficient
(D) EACH statement ALONE is sufficient
(E) Statements (1) and (2) TOGETHER are NOT sufficient

Following the question are **two
Statements** labeled (1) and (2).

To answer Data Sufficiency problems
correctly, you need to decide **whether
the statements provide enough
information to answer the question.**
In other words, do you have
sufficient data?

Lastly, you are given the **Answer Choices.**

These are the *same* for every Data Sufficiency problem so
memorize them as soon as possible.

The question stem contains the question you need to answer. The two statements provide *given* information, information that is true. DS questions look strange but you can think of them as deconstructed Problem Solving (PS) questions. Compare the DS-format problem above to the PS-format problem below:

Samuel is 4 years younger than Dmitry, and Samuel will be 11 years old in 5 years.
If Oliver is twice as old as Dmitry, how old is Oliver?

The two questions contain exactly the same information; that information is just presented in a different order. The PS question stem contains all of the givens as well as the question. The DS problem moves some of the givens down to statement (1) and statement (2).

As with regular PS problems, the given information in the DS statements is always true. In addition, the two statements won't contradict each other. In the same way that a PS question wouldn't tell you that $x > 0$ *and* $x < 0$, the two DS statements won't do that either.

In the PS format, you would go ahead and calculate Oliver's age. The DS format works a bit differently. Here is the full problem, including the answer choices:

If Oliver is twice as old as Dmitry, how old is Oliver?

(1) Samuel is 4 years younger than Dmitry.
(2) Samuel will be 11 years old in 5 years.

(A) Statement (1) ALONE is sufficient, but statement (2) is NOT sufficient.
(B) Statement (2) ALONE is sufficient, but statement (1) is NOT sufficient.
(C) BOTH statements TOGETHER are sufficient, but NEITHER statement ALONE is
    sufficient.
(D) EACH statement ALONE is sufficient.
(E) Statements (1) and (2) TOGETHER are NOT sufficient.

Despite all appearances, the question is not actually asking you to calculate Oliver's age. Rather, it's asking *which pieces of information* would allow you to calculate Oliver's age.

You may already be able solve this one on your own, but you'll see much harder problems on the test, so your first task is to learn how to work through DS questions in a systematic, consistent way.

As you think the problem through, jot down information from the question stem:

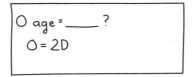

Hmm. If they tell you Dmitry's age, then you can find Oliver's age. Remember that!

Take a look at the first statement. Also, write down the $\frac{AD}{BCE}$ answer grid (you'll learn why as you work through the problem):

(1) Samuel is 4 years younger than Dmitry.

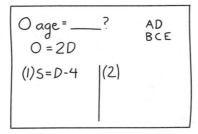

The first statement doesn't allow you to figure out anyone's real age. Statement (1), then, is *not sufficient*. Now you can cross off the top row of answers, (A) and (D).

Why? Here's the text for answers (A) and (D):

(A) Statement (1) ALONE is sufficient, but statement (2) is NOT sufficient.
(D) EACH statement ALONE is sufficient.

Both answers indicate that statement (1) is sufficient to answer the question. Because statement (1) is *not* sufficient to find Oliver's age, both (A) and (D) are wrong.

The answer choices will always appear in the order shown for the above problem, so any time you decide that statement (1) is not sufficient, you will always cross off answers (A) and (D). That's why your answer grid groups these two answers together.

Next, consider statement (2), but remember one tricky thing: forget what statement (1) told you. Because of the way DS is constructed, you must evaluate the two statements separately before you look at them together:

    (2) Samuel will be 11 years old in 5 years.

It's useful to write the two statements side-by-side, as shown above, to help remember that statement (2) is separate from statement (1) and has to be considered by itself first.

Statement (2) does indicate how old Sam is now, but says nothing about Oliver or Dmitry. (Remember, you're looking *only* at statement (2) now.) By itself, statement (2) is not sufficient, so cross off answer (B).

Now that you've evaluated each statement by itself, take a look at the two statements together. Statement (2) provides Sam's age, and statement (1) allows you to calculate Dmitry's age if you know Sam's age. Finally, the question stem allows you to calculate Oliver's age if you know Dmitry's age:

As soon as you can tell that you *can* solve, put down a check mark or write an S with a circle around it (or both!). Don't actually calculate Oliver's age; the GMAT doesn't give you any extra time to calculate a number that you don't need.

The correct answer is **(C)**.

The Answer Choices

The five Data Sufficiency answer choices will always be exactly the same (and presented in the same order), so memorize them before you go into the test.

Here are the five answers written in an easier way to understand:

> (A) Statement (1) does allow you to answer the question, but statement (2) does not.
> (B) Statement (2) does allow you to answer the question, but statement (1) does not.
> (C) Neither statement works on its own, but you can use them *together* to answer the question.
> (D) Statement (1) works by itself *and* statement (2) works by itself.
> (E) Nothing works. Even if you use both statements together, you still can't answer the question.

Answer (C) specifically says that neither statement works on its own. For this reason, you are required to look at each statement by itself *and decide that neither one works* before you are allowed to evaluate the two statements together.

Here's an easier way to remember the five answer choices; we call this the "twelve-ten" mnemonic (memory aid):

1	only statement 1
2	only statement 2
T	together
E	either one
N	neither/nothing

Within the next week, memorize the DS answers. If you do a certain number of practice DS problems in that time frame, you'll likely memorize the answers without conscious effort—and you'll solidify the DS lessons you're learning right now.

Starting with Statement (2)

If statement (1) looks hard, start with statement (2) instead. Your process will be the same, except you'll make one change in your answer grid.

Try this problem:

> If Oliver is twice as old as Dmitry, how old is Oliver?
>
> (1) Two years ago, Dmitry was twice as old as Samuel.
> (2) Samuel is 6 years old.

(From now on, the answer choices won't be shown. Start memorizing!)

Statement (1) is definitely more complicated than statement (2), so start with statement (2) instead. Change your answer grid to $\begin{matrix} BD \\ ACE \end{matrix}$. (You'll learn why in a minute.)

(2) Samuel is 6 years old.

Statement (2) is not sufficient to determine Oliver's age, so cross off the answers that say statement (2) is sufficient: (B) and (D). Once again, you can cross off the entire top row; when starting with statement (2), you always will keep or eliminate these two choices at the same time.

Now assess statement (1):

(1) Two years ago, Dmitry was twice as old as Samuel.

Forget all about statement (2); only statement (1) exists. By itself, is the statement sufficient?

Nope! Too many variables. Cross off (A), the first of the remaining answers in the bottom row, and assess the two statements together:

You can plug Samuel's age (from the second statement) into the formula from statement (1) to find Dmitry's age, and then use Dmitry's age to find Oliver's age. Together, the statements are sufficient.

The correct answer is **(C)**.

The two answer grids work in the same way, regardless of which one you use. As long as you use the AD/BCE grid when starting with statement (1), or the BD/ACE grid when starting with statement (2), you will always:

- cross off the *top* row if the first statement you try is *not* sufficient;
- cross off the *bottom* row if the first statement you try *is* sufficient; and
- assess the remaining row of answers one answer at a time.

Finally, remember that you must assess the statements separately before you can try them together—and you'll only try them together if neither one is sufficient on its own. You will only consider the two together if you have already crossed off answers (A), (B), and (D).

Value vs. Yes/No Questions

Data Sufficiency questions come in two "flavors": Value or Yes/No.

On Value questions, it is necessary to find a single value in order to answer the question. If you can't find any value or you can find two or more values, then the information is not sufficient.

Consider this statement:

> (1) Oliver's age is a multiple of 4.

Oliver could be 4 or 8 or 12 or any age that is a multiple of 4. Because it's impossible to determine one particular value for Oliver's age, the statement is not sufficient

What if the question changed?

> Is Oliver's age an even number?
>
> (1) Oliver's age is a multiple of 4.
> (2) Oliver is between 19 and 23 years old.

This question is a Yes/No question. There are three possible answers to a Yes/No question:

1. Always Yes: Sufficient!
2. Always No: Sufficient!
3. Maybe (or Sometimes Yes, Sometimes No): Not Sufficient

It may surprise you that Always No is sufficient to answer the question. Imagine that you ask a friend to go to the movies with you. If she says, "No, I'm sorry, I can't," then you did receive an answer to your question (even though the answer is negative). You know she can't go to the movies with you.

Apply this reasoning to the Oliver question. Is statement 1 sufficient to answer the question *Is Oliver's age an even number?*

> (1) Oliver's age is a multiple of 4.

If Oliver's age is a multiple of 4, then Yes, he must be an even number of years old. The information isn't enough to tell how old Oliver actually is—he could be 4, 8, 12, or any multiple of 4 years old. Still, the information is sufficient to answer the specific question asked.

Because the statement tried first is sufficient, cross off the bottom row of answers, (B), (C), and (E).

Next, check statement (2):

> (2) Oliver is between 19 and 23 years old.

Oliver could be 20, in which case his age is even. He could also be 21, in which case his age is odd. The answer here is Sometimes Yes, Sometimes No, so the information is not sufficient to answer the question.

The correct answer is **(A)**: the first statement is sufficient but the second is not.

The DS Process

This section summarizes everything you've learned in one consistent DS process. You can use this on every DS problem on the test.

Step 1: Determine whether the question is Value or Yes/No.

Value: The question asks for the value of an unknown (e.g., What is x?).

A statement is **Sufficient** when it provides **1 possible value**.

A statement is **Not Sufficient** when it provides **more than 1 possible value** (or none at all).

Yes/No: The question asks whether a given piece of information is true (e.g., Is x even?). Most of the time, these will be in the form of Yes/No questions.

A statement is **Sufficient** when the answer is **Always Yes** or **Always No**.

A statement is **Not Sufficient** when the answer is **Maybe** or **Sometimes Yes, Sometimes No**.

Step 2: Separate given information from the question itself.

If the question stem contains given information—that is, any information other than the question itself—then write down that information separately from the question itself. This is true information that you must consider or use when answering the question.

Step 3: Rephrase the question.

Most of the time, you will not write down the entire question stem exactly as it appears on screen. At the least, you'll simplify what is written on screen. For example, if the question stem asks, "What is the value of x?" then you might write down something like $x = \underline{\hspace{2cm}}$?

For more complicated question stems, you may have more work to do. Ideally, before you go to the statements, you will be able to articulate a fairly clear and straightforward question. In the earlier example, $x = \underline{\hspace{2cm}}$? is clear and straightforward.

What if this is the question?

> If $xyz \neq 0$, is $\dfrac{3x}{2} + y + 2z = \dfrac{7x}{2} + y$?
>
> (1) $y = 3$ and $x = 2$
> (2) $z = -x$

Do you need to know the individual values of x, y, and z in order to answer the question? Would knowing the value of a combination of the variables, such as $x + y + z$, work? It's tough to tell.

In order to figure this out, **rephrase** the question stem, which is a fancy way of saying: simplify the information a lot. Take the time to do this before you address the statements; you'll make your job much easier!

If you're given an equation, the first task is to put the "like" variables together. Also, when working with the question stem, make sure to carry the question mark through your work:

$$y - y + 2z = \frac{7x}{2} - \frac{3x}{2}?$$

That's interesting: the two y variables cancel out. Keep simplifying:

$$2z = \frac{4x}{2}?$$
$$2z = 2x?$$
$$z = x?$$

That whole crazy equation is really asking a much simpler question: is $z = x$?

It might seem silly to keep writing that question mark at the end of each line, but don't skip that step or you'll be opening yourself up to a careless error. By the time you get to the end, you don't want to forget that this is still a *question*, not a statement or given.

Step 4: Use the Answer Grid to Evaluate the Statements

If you start with statement 1, then write the AD/BCE grid on your scrap paper.

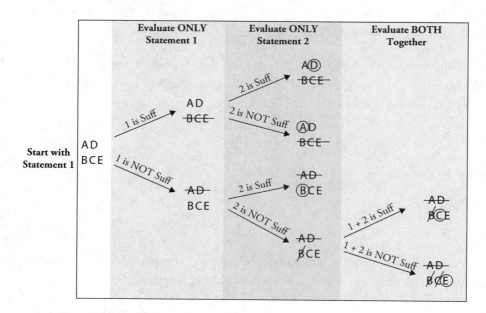

Here is the rephrased problem:

     If $xyz \neq 0$, is $z = x$?

     (1) $y = 3$ and $x = 2$

     (2) $z = -x$

Statement (1) is useless by itself because it says nothing about z. Cross off the top row of answers: $\dfrac{\text{AD}}{\text{BCE}}$

Statement (2) turns out to be very useful. None of the variables is 0, so if $z = -x$, then those two numbers cannot be equal to each other. This statement is sufficient to answer the question: no, z does not equal x. You can circle B on your grid: $\dfrac{\text{AD}}{\text{BCE}}$

The correct answer is (B).

MANHATTAN
PREP

If you decide to start with statement (2), your process is almost identical, but you'll use the BD/ACE grid instead. For example:

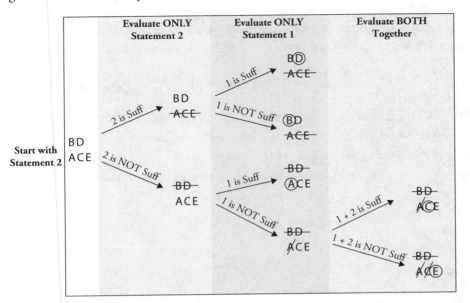

First, evaluate statement (1) by itself and, if you've crossed off answers (A), (B), and (D), then evaluate the two statements together.

Whether you use AD/BCE or BD/ACE, remember to

- cross off the *top* row if the first statement you try is *not* sufficient, and
- cross off the *bottom* row if the first statement you try *is* sufficient.

Pop Quiz! Test Your Skills

Have you learned the DS process? If not, go back through the chapter and work through the sample problems again. Try writing out each step yourself.

If so, prove it! Give yourself up to four minutes total to try the following two problems:

1. Are there more engineers than salespeople working at SoHo Corp?

    (1) SoHo Corp employs $\frac{2}{3}$ as many clerical staff as engineers and salespeople combined.

    (2) If 3 more engineers were employed by SoHo Corp and the number of salespeople remained the same, then the number of engineers would be double the number of salespeople employed by the company.

2. At SoHo Corp, what is the ratio of managers to non-managers?

(1) If there were 3 more managers and the number of salespeople remained the same, then the ratio of managers to non-managers would double.
(2) There are 4 times as many non-managers as managers at SoHo Corp.

How did it go? Are you very confident in your answers? Somewhat confident? Not at all confident?

Before you check your answers, go back over your work, using the DS process discussed in this chapter as your guide. Where can you improve? Did you write down (and use!) your answer grid? Did you look at each statement separately before looking at them together (if necessary)? Did you mix up any of the steps of the process? How neat is the work on your scrap paper? You may want to rewrite your work before you review the answers.

Pop Quiz Answer Key

1. Engineers vs. Salespeople

Step 1: Is this a Value or Yes/No question?

1. Are there more engineers than salespeople working at SoHo Corp?

This is a Yes/No question.

Steps 2 and 3: What is given and what is the question? Rephrase the question.

The question stem doesn't contain any given information. In this case, the question is already about as simplified as it can get: are there more engineers than salespeople?

Step 4: Evaluate the statements.

If you start with the first statement, use the AD/BCE answer grid.

(1) SoHo Corp employs $\frac{2}{3}$ as many clerical staff as engineers and salespeople combined.

If you add up the engineers and salespeople, then there are fewer people on the clerical staff…but this indicates nothing about the relative number of engineers and salespeople. This statement is not sufficient. Cross off (A) and (D), the top row, of your answer grid.

(2) If 3 more engineers were employed by SoHo Corp and the number of salespeople remained the same, then the number of engineers would be double the number of salespeople employed by the company.

This one sounds promising. If you add only 3 engineers, then you'll have twice as many engineers as salespeople. Surely, that means there are more engineers than salespeople?

Don't jump to any conclusions. Test some possible numbers; think about fairly extreme scenarios. What if you start with just 1 engineer? When you add 3, you'll have 4 engineers. If there are 4 engineers, then there are half as many, or 2, salespeople. In other words, you start with 1 engineer and 2 salespeople, so there are more salespeople. Interesting.

According to this one case, the answer to the Yes/No question *Are there more engineers than salespeople?* is no.

Can you find a yes answer? Try a larger set of numbers. If you start with 11 engineers and add 3, then you would have 14 total. The number of salespeople would have to be 7. In this case, then, there are more engineers to start than salespeople, so the answer to the question *Are there more engineers than salespeople?* is yes.

Because you can find both yes and no answers, statement (2) is not sufficient. Cross off answer (B).

Now, try the two statements together. How does the information about the clerical staff combine with statement (2)?

Whenever you're trying some numbers and you have to examine the two statements together, see whether you can reuse the numbers that you tried earlier.

If you start with 1 engineer, you'll have 2 salespeople, for a total of 3. In this case, you'd have 2 clerical staff, and the answer to the original question is no.

If you start with 11 engineers, you'll have 7 salespeople, for a total of 18. In this case, you'd have 12 clerical staff, and the answer to the original question is yes.

The correct answer is **(E)**. The information is not sufficient even when both statements are used together.

2. Managers vs. Non-Managers

Step 1: Is this a Value or a Yes/No question?

> 2. At SoHo Corp, what is the ratio of managers to non-managers?

This is a Value question. You need to find one specific ratio—or know that you can find one specific ratio—in order to answer the question.

Steps 2 and 3: What is given and what is the question? Rephrase the question.

Find the ratio of managers to non-managers, or $M:N$.

Step 4: Evaluate the statements.

If you start with the second statement, use the BD/ACE answer grid. (Note: this is always your choice; the solution with the BD/ACE grid shown is just for practice.)

> (2) There are 4 times as many non-managers as managers at SoHo Corp.

If there is 1 manager, there are 4 non-managers. If there are 2 managers, there are 8 non-managers. If there are 3 managers, there are 12 non-managers.

What does that mean? In each case, the ratio of managers to non-managers is the same, 1:4. Even though you don't know how many managers and non-managers there are, you do know the ratio. (For more on ratios, see the Ratios chapter of the *Fractions, Decimals, & Percents GMAT Strategy Guide*.)

This statement is sufficient; cross (A), (C), and (E), the bottom row, off of the grid.

> (1) If there were 3 more managers and the number of salespeople remained the same,
>   then the ratio of managers to non-managers would double.

First, what does it mean to *double* a ratio? If the starting ratio were 2:3, then doubling that ratio would give you 4:3. The first number in the ratio doubles relative to the second number.

Test some cases. If you start with 1 manager, then 3 more would bring the total number of managers to 4. The *manager* part of the ratio just quadrupled (1 to 4), not doubled, so this number is not a valid starting point. Discard this case.

If you have to add 3 and want that number to double, then you need to start with 3 managers. When you add 3 more, that portion of the ratio doubles from 3 to 6. The other portion, the non-managers, remains the same.

Notice anything? The statement says nothing about the relative number of non-managers. The starting ratio could be 3:2 or 3:4 or 3:14, for all you know. In each case, doubling the number of managers would double the ratio (to 6:2, or 6:4, or 6:14). You can't figure out the specific ratio from this statement.

The correct answer is **(B)**: statement (2) is sufficient, but statement (1) is not.

Proving Insufficiency

The Pop Quiz solutions used the Testing Cases strategy: testing real numbers to help determine whether a statement is sufficient. You can do this whenever the problem allows for the possibility of multiple numbers or cases.

When you're doing this, your goal is to try to prove the statement insufficient. For example:

> If x and y are positive integers, is the sum of x and y between 20 and 26, inclusive?
>
> (1) $x - y = 6$

Test your first case. You're allowed to pick any numbers for x and y that make statement 1 true *and* that follow any constraints given in the question stem. In this case, that means the two numbers have to be positive integers and that $x - y$ has to equal 6.

Case #1: $20 - 14 = 6$. These numbers make statement 1 true and follow the constraint in the question stem, so these are legal numbers to pick. Now, try to answer the Yes/No question: $20 + 14 = 34$, so no, the sum is not between 20 and 26, inclusive.

You now have a *no* answer. Can you think of another set of numbers that will give you the opposite, a *yes* answer?

Case #2: $15 - 9 = 6$. In this case, the sum is 24, so the answer to the Yes/No question is yes, the sum is between 20 and 26, inclusive.

Because you have found both a yes and a no answer, the statement is not sufficient.

Here's a summary of the process:

1. Notice that you can test cases. You can do this when the problem allows for multiple possible values.

2. Pick numbers that make the statement true and that follow any givens in the question stem. If you realize that you picked numbers that make the statement false or contradict givens in the question stem, *discard* those numbers and start over.

3. Your first case will give you one answer: a yes or a no on a Yes/No problem, or a numerical value on a value problem.

4. Try to find a second case that gives you a *different* answer. On a Yes/No problem, you'll be looking for the opposite of what you found for the first case. For a Value problem, you'll be looking for a different numerical answer. (Don't forget that whatever you pick still has to make the statement true and follow the givens in the question stem!)

The usefulness of trying to prove insufficiency is revealed as soon as you find two different answers. You're done! That statement is not sufficient, so you can cross off an answer or answers and move to the next step.

What if you keep finding the same answer? Try this:

> If x and y are positive integers, is the product of x and y between 20 and 26, inclusive?
>
> (1) x is a multiple of 17.

Case #1: Test $x = 17$. Since y must be a positive integer, try the smallest possible value first: $y = 1$. In this case, the product is 17, which is not between 20 and 26 inclusive. The answer to the question is *no*; can you find the opposite answer?

Case #2: If you make $x = 34$, then xy will be too big, so keep $x = 17$. The next smallest possible value for y is 2. In this case, the product is 34, which is also not between 20 and 26 inclusive. The answer is again no.

Can you think of a case where you will get a *yes* answer? No! The smallest possible product is 17, and the next smallest possible product is 34. Any additional values of x and y you try will be equal to or larger than 34.

You've just proved the statement sufficient because it is impossible to find a yes answer. Testing Cases can help you to figure out the "theory" answer, or the mathematical reasoning that proves the statement is sufficient.

This won't always work so cleanly. Sometimes, you'll keep getting all no answers or all yes answers but you won't be able to figure out the theory behind it all. If you test three or four different cases, and you're actively seeking out the opposite answer but never find it, then go ahead and assume that the statement is sufficient, even if you're not completely sure why.

Do make sure that you're trying numbers with different characteristics. Try both even and odd. Try a prime number. Try zero or a negative or a fraction. (You can only try numbers that are allowed by the problem, of course. In the case of the above problems, you were only allowed to try positive integers.)

Here's how Testing Cases would work on a Value problem:

> If x and y are prime numbers, what is the product of x and y?
>
> (1) The product is even.

Case #1: $x = 2$ and $y = 3$. Both numbers are prime numbers and their product is even, so these are legal numbers to try. In this case, the product is 6. Can you choose numbers that will give a different product?

Case #2: $x = 2$ and $y = 5$. Both numbers are prime numbers and their product is even, so these are legal numbers to try. In this case, the product is 10.

The statement is not sufficient because there are at least two different values for the product of x and y.

In short, when you're evaluating DS statements, go into them with an "I'm going to try to prove you insufficient!" mindset.

- If you do find two different answers (yes and no, or two different numbers), then immediately declare that statement not sufficient.

- If, after several tries, you keep finding the same answer despite trying different kinds of numbers, see whether you can articulate why; that statement may be sufficient after all. Even if you can't say why, go ahead and assume that the statement is sufficient.

Now you're ready to test your Data Sufficiency skills. As you work through the chapters in this book, test your progress using some of the *Official Guide* problem set lists found online in your Manhattan Prep Student Center. Start with lower-numbered problems first, in order to practice the process, and work your way up to more and more difficult problems.

mba Mission

EVERY CANDIDATE HAS A STORY TO TELL.
We have the creative experience to help you tell yours.

We are mbaMission, a professional MBA admissions consulting firm, specializing in helping business school applicants identify and showcase the strongest aspects of their candidacy in their applications. Our dedicated senior consultants—all published authors with elite MBA experience—will work one-on-one with you to help you discover, select and articulate your unique stories and force the admissions committees to take notice.

All Manhattan GMAT students enrolled in a complete program receive

- Free 30-minute consultation with an mbaMission senior consultant – Sign up at www.mbamission.com/consult.php
- Free copy of our 250-page book, *The Complete Start-to-Finish MBA Admissions Guide,* loaded with application advice as well as sample essays, recommendations, resumes and more
- One free Insider's Guide on one of 16 top business schools (available in the Manhattan GMAT Student Center)

mbaMission Services

- **Complete Start-to-Finish Package** offers unlimited service for a flat fee and guides you through the entire MBA application process, from brainstorming and outlining to interviews and beyond
- **A la Carte Hourly Services** focus on specific application needs, such as perfecting a single essay, reviewing your resume or analyzing a recommendation
- **Mock Interview Sessions** simulate a real MBA interview with feedback
- **MBA Application Boot Camp** demonstrates how to create a standout application in a live, classroom "workshop" environment

www.mbamission.com/manhattangmat | info@mbamission.com | (646) 485-8844

GO BEYOND BOOKS.
TRY A FREE CLASS NOW.

IN-PERSON COURSE

Find a GMAT course near you and attend the first session free, no strings attached. You'll meet your instructor, learn how the GMAT is scored, review strategies for Data Sufficiency, dive into Sentence Correction, and gain insights into a wide array of GMAT principles and strategies.

Find your city at manhattanprep.com/gmat/classes

ONLINE COURSE

Enjoy the flexibility of prepping from home or the office with our online course. Your instructor will cover all the same content and strategies as an in-person course, while giving you the freedom to prep where you want. Attend the first session free to check out our cutting-edge online classroom.

See the full schedule at manhattanprep.com/gmat/classes

GMAT® INTERACT™

GMAT Interact is a comprehensive self-study program that is fun, intuitive, and driven by you. Each interactive video lesson is taught by an expert instructor and can be accessed on your computer or mobile device. Lessons are personalized for you based on the choices you make.

Try 5 full lessons for free at manhattanprep.com/gmat/interact

Not sure which is right for you? Try all three! Or give us a call and we'll help you figure out which program fits you best.

Toll-Free U.S. Number (800) 576-4628 | **International** 001 (212) 721-7400 | **Email** gmat@manhattanprep.com

PRΣP MADE PΣRSONAL

Whether you want quick coaching
in a particular GMAT subject area
or a comprehensive study plan developed
around your goals, we've got you covered.
Our expert, 99th percentile GMAT tutors
can help you hit your top score.

CHECK OUT THESE REVIEWS FROM MANHATTAN PREP TUTORING STUDENTS.

Highly Recommend MGMAT for a 700 Score
★★★★★ *June 1, 2014*

Company: Manhattan GMAT *296 reviews*
Course: Manhattan GMAT Private Tutoring *24 reviews*
GMAT Scores — Before: 680 **After:** 720

reviews.beatthegmat.com

I bought the MGMAT books and started studying on my own. Along with using the MGMAT materials I also met with a Manhattan private tutor. He was fantastic. He really listed to my concerns and tried to understand what was holding me back. He's very down to earth and pragmatic. Not only did he help me understand the test material better, he helped me to have a better mental game while taking it. After meeting with him and studying with the MGMAT materials I boosted my score to a 720.

Best Prep Out There!
★★★★★

Company: Manhattan GMAT *296 reviews*
Course: Manhattan GMAT Private Tutoring *24 reviews*
GMAT Scores — Before: 560 **After:** 750

reviews.beatthegmat.com

I just took my GMAT and scored a 750 (Q49, V42). This was a pretty amazing feat for me considering I scored only 560 my first time taking the GMAT. Only by sitting down with the Manhattan GMAT books and really learning the content contained in them was I able to get into the 700 range. Then, when I was consistently scoring in the 90+ percentile, Manhattan tutoring got me my 750 and into the 98th percentile. If you want a 700+ on the GMAT, use Manhattan GMAT. PERIOD!!

A one-hour private tutoring session took me to the next level.
★★★★★

Company: Manhattan GMAT *296 reviews*
Course: Manhattan GMAT Private Tutoring *24 reviews*
GMAT Scores — Before: N/A **After:** 730

reviews.beatthegmat.com

I purchased the MGMAT materials second-hand and pursued a self-study strategy. I was stuck between 700 and 720 on all my practice exams, but was hoping to get into the mid-700s. I thought a private tutoring session would really help me go to the next level in my scoring. [My instructor] asked me beforehand (via email) what I was struggling with and what I thought I needed. Marc was able to quickly talk me through my struggles and give me concise, helpful tips that I used during the remainder of my study time and the actual exam.

Manhattan GMAT is Best in Class
★★★★★

Company: Manhattan GMAT *296 reviews*
Course: Manhattan GMAT Private Tutoring *24 reviews*
GMAT Scores — Before: N/A **After:** 750

reviews.beatthegmat.com

I signed up for the self study so that I could review the materials on my own time. After completing the basic course content and taking a couple practice tests I signed up for private tutoring. Andrea helped me to develop a game plan to address my weaknesses. We discussed the logic behind the problem and practical strategies for eliminating certain answers if time is running short. Originally I had planned on taking the GMAT two times. But, MGMAT and Andrea helped me to exceed my goal on the first attempt, allowing me to focus on the rest of my application.

CALL OR EMAIL US AT **800-576-4628** OR **GMAT@MANHATTANPREP.COM**
FOR INFORMATION ON RATES AND TO GET PAIRED WITH YOUR GMAT TUTOR.